In The Red

Alexis Hall

In The Red

The diary of a recovering shopaholic

ICON BOOKS

Published in the UK in 2008 by
Icon Books Ltd, The Old Dairy, Brook Road,
Thriplow, Cambridge SG8 7RG
email: info@iconbooks.co.uk
www.iconbooks.co.uk

Sold in the UK, Europe, South Africa and Asia
by Faber & Faber Ltd, 3 Queen Square,
London WC1N 3AU or their agents

Distributed in the UK, Europe, South Africa and Asia
by TBS Ltd, TBS Distribution Centre, Colchester Road
Frating Green, Colchester CO7 7DW

This edition published in Australia in 2007
by Allen & Unwin Pty Ltd, PO Box 8500,
83 Alexander Street, Crows Nest, NSW 2065

Distributed in Canada by Penguin Books Canada,
90 Eglinton Avenue East, Suite 700,
Toronto, Ontario M4P 2YE

ISBN: 978-1840468-60-1

Typeset in 12 on 14.5pt Minion by Marie Doherty

Printed and bound in the UK by
Creative Print and Design Group

Contents

About the author

Alexis Hall is a media relations officer and former broadcast journalist. She lives in Glasgow with her partner, their four-legged, furry child and her large collection of shoes. *In the Red* is her first book.

Acknowledgements

Patience, encouragement and love made this book possible and those who gave it know who they are ...

Introduction

How did it come to this?

Thirty-one thousand, six hundred and thirty-seven pounds and eighty-four pence.

That's how much money I owe.

Even saying it quickly doesn't make it sound any better.

It's the first time I've ever sat down and added it all up to the very last penny and I feel physically sick looking at the display on the calculator. I try turning it upside down to see if that helps. It looks like 'hOLEgIE', which probably means 'loser' in some long-forgotten language. Perhaps I should have it tattooed on my arm in Sanskrit.

The trouble is I'm a shopaholic and as far as I can remember, I've always been like this.

Even as a child, I would stand blubbing and snorting in the newsagent's shop because I wanted something, anything. It was hardly Hamleys and as we went in there every morning to collect the paper, I'm stumped as to what I could have wanted that badly on a daily basis.

For me, the slide into debt probably all started when I was a student, away from home and entrusted with a £500 overdraft. Like any addiction, my spending started off being fun, manageable and a bit of a thrill.

However impossible it may seem to take the leap from £500 to over £30,000, when you consider that it's taken me twenty years to run up that level of debt, it means I've really only been adding on just over £1,500 a year. Suddenly it seems easy …

And it's even easier when you have no problem getting credit. I'm not making excuses for myself by saying I should never have been allowed to get to this stage, but so far, no one's put the brakes on my runaway financial Ferrari.

I'd have no problem getting my grabbing little mitts on another few thousand before the refusal letters started to come through. If you're smart, you make sure that you pay a little extra to your bills every month, so you never get a bad credit rating. That way the credit cards and loans just keep on coming.

Each one you get will be the last one and you promise yourself you'll only use it in an emergency. Two months later, you've maxed the card out and don't know where you'll get the money to pay it back.

How depressing … never mind, you can always go shopping to cheer yourself up. And round we go again …

I suppose like any addict, you can only start recovering once you admit you have a problem and the time has come for me to do that. To stand up and say: 'My name is Alexis and I'm a compulsive spender.'

My massive debt is stretched across four credit cards and two loans. On both occasions, the loans were taken out to clear the credit cards. Instead of then closing the accounts, I kept the cards in a 'safe place', which evidently wasn't safe enough, as I ran them all back up to their limit again. Each time I did that, my disposable income was cut even further in order for me to make the payments, leaving me with even less cash.

I'd like to point out at this stage that I don't even own a car and my debt doesn't include my half of the mortgage, which I share with my partner, Kevin.

Kevin really is the original long-suffering partner. He's put up with me and my compulsive spending for nearly fourteen years. He once paid off all my credit cards and made me stand at the bin with a pair of scissors cutting up my plastic partners in crime. He listened to me sobbing and wailing, promising I'd never do it again and I've thanked him by running the whole lot up to the hilt again.

So, what have I spent the money on? What do I have to show for this mountain of debt? In fact, pathetically little.

I can't even claim to have a wardrobe bursting with haute couture, although I do admit to a hefty collection of Mulberry bags, a few pairs of Gina and Prada shoes and, rather bizarrely, four evening dresses – all in black, all but one unworn.

Actually, most of my clothes are unworn. They languish unloved in a heap at the bottom of the wardrobe, screwed up and shoved shamelessly in drawers, or worst of all neatly folded in the bags and boxes they came in, complete with tags to remind me of their awful cost.

On more than one occasion, I've even come across items I've bought twice, unaware that I already owned the piece I was so proud to have purchased.

And it's all about the purchase. That exquisite moment when the object of your desire suddenly becomes yours.

After that it all goes downhill. Mainly because of the guilt – guilt that you shouldn't have bought it, guilt that you'll have to lie to your partner, either by hiding it and pretending it doesn't exist, or by using the classic line: 'That old thing? I've had it for ages. Don't you remember when I wore it to …?'

Guilt leads to glum moods and glum moods lead to a quick trip to the shops to get back the 'high' from the initial purchase.

I've even been known to fall for 'purchasing for profit' schemes: buying a load of stuff that I think I'll off-load at a later date, making wads of cash in the process.

The best example of this was when I first heard a band called Franz Ferdinand. I knew, just knew, they were going to be the next big thing, so started buying up as much of their merchandise as possible. Signed, rare, white label …

Having amassed around £700 worth, I then decided that I rather liked the band myself and set out to buy doubles, so I could sell one lot and keep my own collection too.

Of course, they were the next big thing, but I didn't sell on my goods quickly enough. The prices plummeted and I was left with two shelves full of Franz, mocking me and my monetary mistake.

I've known for a while that I couldn't continue like this and since the start of the year, I've been trying to psych myself up for going cold turkey on consumerism – but something always gets in the way.

Like the £100 iron that would solve all of our ironing issues and reduce the EU ironing mountain that lives in our study. It certainly gets the ironing done quicker, but has highlighted the fact that I simply don't have enough space for all of my clothes.

They now lie in neatly ironed piles on top of a six-foot long chest of drawers – the entire surface of which is covered with teetering mounds almost two feet tall, threatening to topple over and smother us as we sleep. Death by designer label!

Then there was last week's little trip to Rome for Kevin's 40th birthday, where we spent seven decadent days in one of the city's top hotels, living like lords and shopping to suit.

Let's face it, you can't help but go crazy in a city where they sell live lobster in the SPAR. My intention was that throughout the trip, Kevin would want for nothing and pay for nothing. That was never going to be cheap, but can you really put a price on a partner's happiness and doing something special for their big four-o?

Besides it's nice to come home and realise that the white, Italian leather loafers, although so impractical in the British weather, were a white-hot hit as you sipped limoncello and smoked Café Crème by the Colosseum.

I'd been saving for the trip for over a year and deep down I think I knew this was going to be my last chance to really splash out.

But back to reality, bills and the realisation that now more than ever, the time is ripe for recompense.

Don't think that I haven't tried to analyse the rationale behind my lack of control; my compulsion to buy things I don't need, don't always want and definitely can't afford.

Did I have an unhappy childhood? Did something traumatic happen to me that I can't get over? Was I just thoroughly spoiled and am now unable to accept that I can't have everything?

To be honest, I could probably answer a tentative 'yes' to all of those questions, but it doesn't change the situation now. Probing the past may provide me with some clues as to why

I behave the way I do, but for the time being it isn't going to magic away the minus sign on my bank balance. Only self-control and a curb on my spending can do that.

So, do I lie on a shrink's couch talking until the cows come home, digging myself an even deeper hole as I search for the definitive answer or do I just face up to the fact that I'm ruining my life – and that of those closest to me – with the burden of debt?

'Ruining' might seem a bid heavy-handed, but it's not. I can't begin to count the number of times I've had to decline invitations to dinner, parties, the theatre, trips away – all because I couldn't afford to go and still make the payments needed to stop me being blacklisted. I've been so busy trying to buy the life I think I should be living, that I can't afford to live the one I have.

It wouldn't be so bad if it just affected me, but it's limiting Kevin's options too. If I can't afford to do something, it means we either shelve the whole thing or he has to pay my share, which hardly seems fair when we're both earning the same.

Desperately seeking an answer, I've read numerous self-help books and articles relating to debt and shopping, but they've given me nothing more than an insight to a world I can't relate to.

Half of them seemed to have been written by people who, although happy to wield a little purchasing power now and then, didn't even come close to being bracketed in the same 'serial shopper' category as myself. For them, there appeared to be no dilemmas about having to choose which colour of shoes to buy, before heading home with two or three pairs because the choice was just too painful.

Then there were the pieces penned by those with no debt, serious amounts of savings and a desire to simply drop out of the consumer cycle, head off into the woods and live like hermits.

I don't want to lock myself away and recycle leftover bits of soap, I just want to clear my debt and learn a little self-control and surely I can't be the only one? The average thirty-something female Brit owes over £8,200. Bridget Jones is on the verge of going bust!

We're a nation of debtors (Britain's personal debt has now topped the £1 trillion mark) going crazy with our flexible friends, mortgaging ourselves to the hilts and never thinking that one day it'll be payback time. But for me, it is.

I don't want to be buried in a pauper's grave – albeit in a very nice pair of Prada shoes and a Hobbs suit – so I'm taking the next year to rein myself in and see if I can teach myself a little debt discipline.

A year-long experiment in economising without totally depriving myself and the rules are simple.

1. No new clothes, shoes or accessories unless it's a complete emergency, and by emergency I mean discovering that my entire wardrobe has been swept away in an avalanche or I've put holes in the toes of all my socks – whichever happens first.
2. Necessity purchases only – toiletries, food, transport, etc. (limo hire never has been and never will be a necessity).

3. Aim to pay off as much of my debt as possible without using any existing credit cards or applying for new ones.

Seems simple enough. Maybe I'll save nothing and maybe I'll learn nothing, but at this stage, I feel I have nothing more to lose.

But then, even that's not strictly true.

If I don't keep up the loan and credit card repayments, I could lose my house. And let's face it, the roof over my head would seem like a tiny loss in comparison to the damage I could do to the relationships I have with my nearest and dearest. Bricks and mortar are far easier to replace than love, trust and respect.

And so it seems there's a lot more resting on this experiment than simply putting a stop to my compulsive consumerism and seeing a decrease in my debts.

If I can't have new shoes ...

May 2006

Debt to date = £31,637.84

Sunday 14 May – Countdown to D-Day

The eve of my debt detox and already I'm facing a dilemma.

Kevin's announced that he's selling one of his cars. Downsizing to one vehicle isn't an issue, but as I make a habit of blagging the spare one on a daily basis to drive to work, I could be facing a transport problem.

My other options are a train ride 50 minutes before I'm due to start work, followed by a fifteen-minute walk to the office, or trying to figure out which one of several hundred buses gets me nearest to work without going via the moon.

Truth is, I'm scared of buses. They go on routes that I don't recognise or understand, forcing me to get off miles away from my stop in case I go past it and end up in Aberdeen.

Also, it rains a lot in Glasgow, which causes the windows of the bus to steam up. This results in me panicking even more, desperately wiping the glass with my sleeve, trying to see through the smeary mess to the street outside; then giving up, getting off and walking through the thunderstorm to my destination.

Of course, there is another option ...

Less than a week ago we were in Rome, the home of the scooter, and although I'd never considered getting one myself, it makes perfect sense when you live in a city.

I know it's a purchase I can barely justify but it's the perfect solution to my quandary – there are motorbike bays at the front and back of my office, and it would take me a maximum of twenty minutes door to door.

Having checked a few prices online, I've found the second-hand ones are either pricier than some of the new ones or are being sold on sites that leave me thinking I could end up owning a motorised roller skate.

I know it's not the ideal start to twelve months of limited spending, but I'm seeing it as an added challenge, and over a two-year period, the scooter does work out cheaper than taking the train.

The upside is that I'm getting into the economising mentality and thinking about what I can do to raise the money. I've already toyed with the idea of flogging Kevin's golf clubs, but as he seems to be welded to them most of the time, the buyer would probably need to take them both.

Monday 15 May – Day 1

It's the start of the week and (as I see it) the most sensible time to start my experiment.

The rain is bouncing off the pavement, but I can't use the car park near work. Their £13-a-day parking fees are no longer part of my plan and besides, the highwayman's masks their staff wear as they go about their business of daylight robbery are a little scary first thing in the morning.

Instead, I leave a bit earlier than usual and take my chances with the free spaces on the edge of town. I eventually find one and from there it takes me nearly 25 minutes to walk up to my office. I'm soaked when I arrive – but I haven't spend anything.

My morning's daydreaming is split between my perfect scooter and the implications of the Scottish weather on my open-air driving experience. I manage to gloss over the latter.

At lunchtime I take a couple of hundred pounds that I had left over from the Rome trip and put it in the bank. It's been earmarked to buy Harvey Nichols vouchers as a thank you for a friend. This may seem rather extravagant, but when that friend has saved you £1,400 on a hotel bill, you do the right thing.

Last week I'd have pocketed the cash, charged the vouchers to my credit card, then used the money to treat myself to a little something.

Today though, I walk from the bank feeling slightly confused by my actions and slightly cheated out of a shopping spree.

I'm drenched thanks to the walk back to the car after work but elated at having bought nothing but lunch. To celebrate I treat our dog, Hobbs, to an hour of walking and chasing frisbee in what can only be classed as a monsoon.

But I'm happy when I get home and so is he. The water running down my cheeks isn't from the tears that I'd expected to shed as I embarked on a year without excess.

Tuesday 16 May – Day 2
Another day of parking, walking and saving money.

If I can't come up with the money for the scooter, perhaps I could dig out my old bicycle. Somewhere I have all the gear including the clothing, lights and panniers. All I have to do is find it.

This is easier said than done. Years of overspending mean years of excess 'stuff' and trying to find anything is a nightmare. I have no idea where to even start looking and this has made me face the fact that it's not just my spending that needs to be addressed.

I peek into our bedroom (where I suspect my cycling shorts could be hiding) and survey the chaos. Shoes and clothes lie everywhere and none of them are Kevin's. If I were him, I'd leave me!

I look in my wardrobe, which resembles a landfill site, and quickly close the door again. Then I sneak a look in Kevin's side …

His clothes look so much happier than mine! His trousers, neatly folded over their cedar hangers, jostle merrily with shirts that have elbowroom and uncrushed collars, while his shoes sit in perfect rows under coats and suits.

My side's so crushed I've actually had to take shirts off the hanger and iron them again before I could wear them!

Wednesday 17 May – Day 3
I steal myself to go through the pile of bills that were threatening to block the door when we returned from Kevin's birthday break.

I know it's a disgraceful amount of time to leave the mail unopened, but believe me, if you knew what was in my mail, you'd ignore it too.

I grimace as I open each credit card bill, wincing as I realise that the true cost of our Roman holiday may not be truly apparent until next month.

Although I'd saved up for the trip, I still couldn't resist bending my flexible friend so far it practically had a spinal injury.

Then just as I think it can't get any worse, I see them. Tempting me, with images of how perfect my summer could be, are the latest Boden and Jo Malone catalogues.

I stroke their covers and hold the Jo Malone one to my nose to remind me of how the shop smells, but all I get is a whiff of eau de doormat from the time it lay there. I daren't even flick through them, so great is the risk of temptation. Instead I put them in the recycling bin, hoping that next year I'll be able to enter their realms and pages once more.

Thursday 18 May – Day 4

My successful mail sort has led me to go through the internet sites that I've saved as 'favourites'. I delete every one of them!

It's far too tempting to log on and go for a quick mooch in the hope that the £200 item that I covet so much from Toast has been reduced to £15. Of course, if it hasn't, I go through all the other sites until I find something I can justify buying. Two weeks later when said item or items arrive, I've not only completely forgotten purchasing them, but have usually gone off them too.

In anyone else's head that would be the ideal time to return them, but why bother when they can join the rest of the detritus at the bottom of the wardrobe? Why spend the £4 return postage and get the refund, when you can pay the full whack to keep what you don't even want?

That must be the same skewed logic that stops me spending a few pounds to have boots reheeled because it's too pricey, but enables me to justify buying a new pair instead.

Enough said. The shopping sites have to go, along with the companies that I've subscribed to for email updates on their new products. Problem is I can't even remember who they all are, so they'll just have to be dealt with firmly and mercilessly as they crop up.

One joy from yesterday's mail management task was to find that the magazine I subscribe to had been delivered. I buy at least six mags a month, but under the new rules, I'm not allowed.

I leave its pristine pages unopened for now. My usual reading method is a quick skim through the articles (that someone has spent aeons researching) just so I can get to the one page that serves as a directory for all the shops and items featured.

With just one magazine each month, I'm going to have to learn to savour every last word.

Friday 19 May – Day 5

Kevin's car threw a sickie of monumental proportions this morning and after getting the bus into town, he emails me to have a rant.

The breakdown (of the car, not Kevin) isn't such a big deal but he's promised to visit his mum tonight.

She's recently been diagnosed with cancer, so the weekly visits are important to both of them. He usually goes on his own, so they can chat freely about how they both feel and do all of the little silly things that you should do with your parents. Like playing cards and going through old photo albums, laughing at the seventies haircuts and marvelling at Uncle Peter's handlebar moustache. Their latest venture is piecing together the family tree.

I suggest he picks up the car I've brought into town and I'll take the train home. A mini-sacrifice that'll cost me just £1.90.

And it seems karma is on my side, because I get the money back when my friend Alison and I go for coffee a couple of hours later. She picks up the tab, as I'd completely forgotten I paid last time. I keep my purse in my pocket and enjoy my (technically) free caffeine fix.

While we're on the subject of coffee, I know that Rule 2 says I can only purchase things I need and for some, socialising may not fall into that category but for me, friends are a necessity.

I don't have to go crazy and crack open crates of Bollinger every time I see them, but a drink or a cheap meal can be budgeted for and already my friends' support for my experiment is worth its weight in gold.

If I can't have new shoes, at least I can have good company and conversation.

Saturday 20 May – Day 6

I've had one slight dilemma over the past couple of days that appeared in the shape of the lottery.

Again, not a necessity, but as I've played every week since it started and stuck to the same numbers, I'd probably be suicidal with grief if they finally came up and I hadn't bought a ticket.

I could try to avoid the results for a year, but as part of my job involves reading through the newspapers, this would be almost impossible.

It's not so much the cost of the ticket that's the problem. It's more the fact that buying it is a shop-based activity, and I'm almost physically incapable of entering the establishment, parting with my pound and purchasing the ticket alone. There's always a tempting magazine/chocolate bar/bottle of Bombay Sapphire that has to come home with me too.

But, I think I've found the answer. I can buy the ticket online! For the first time ever, I log on, pay the pound and log off.

I'm feeling terribly pleased with myself, mainly because I managed it without crashing the site and screaming like a maniac at the computer (which obviously helps).

All I need to do now is win. Simple really.

(11 pm – Didn't win the lottery. Apparently matching one ball is no use.)

Sunday 21 May – Day 7

Kevin's on a boy's cycling trip this weekend and usually for me, that means a chance to shop unhindered by his rapid-fire remarks.

'How can you afford that bag?' (Visa)

'It's £400!' (It's Fendi)

'Who's really paying for that? You or your credit card?' (Doh!)

I realise this is going to be a real test of my willpower but halfway through the second day, all I've bought is food and all I have to do is keep that frame of mind going. Don't I?

The only problem is that I've been looking forward to a weekend of long, sunny and distracting walks with Hobbs and without my wallet. However, Hobbs has pulled a muscle in his leg and can only go round the block, so I've had to seek alternative and free amusement.

This has come in the form of tidying and hand-washing all of those tedious garments that can't go in the washing machine and spend three-quarters of the year living at the bottom of the laundry basket.

I've even risked the loss of a dry-clean-only raincoat. And when you know that you can't just go out and buy another, believe me, that's a big risk!

Buying the palest of pale trenches seems like a marvellous idea at the time, but when the damn thing looks like it's served in the trenches by the third wear, it starts to lose its lustre.

With a little fear, some delicate washing liquid, a woolwash programme and a lot of faith, it enters the machine and resurfaces just under an hour later – clean, fresh and, most importantly, completely unharmed.

Dare I say it, it's almost therapeutic. It's day seven and already I've turned into Anthea Turner.

Monday 22 May – Day 8

The mail arrives this morning and I pounce on the delicious white envelope with fat silver writing – the Harvey Nicks* vouchers!

I check them over and transfer them to another envelope with my friend's name on it, while doing everything I can to resist the temptation to flee the country with them. I only just manage.

*I worship at the altar of Harvey Nicks, but it's in Edinburgh. This causes a great deal of grief among other like-minded worshippers who see Glasgow as the trendier of the two cities and who were convinced that the divine department store would grace its streets and not those of the capital. Whenever I get the chance to kneel at St Nick's, I make a wish that one day I'll wake up and it will have magically appeared in George Square.

Tuesday 23 May – Day 9

I meet my cousin Verity for coffee. She's expecting her first baby later in the year and so far is unable to convince herself that it's really going to happen.

Her first scan made the baby look like an alien (no, really it did) and having been told that her due date is Hallowe'en, she's understandably feeling a little anxious.

After years of meeting her only at family weddings and funerals, I decided I wanted to get to know her better and it's one of the best things I've done. Every time we meet, I leave in agony from having laughed so hard.

Today the hilarity centres around tales about her famous rock-star neighbour. The story relates to her partner, Stuart, sneaking out the bin bags late at night wearing nothing but his boxer shorts.

Believing that their celebrity neighbour is off touring, Stuart's surprised to see him on the landing and takes part in a short and very embarrassing conversation, before retreating to the flat to find that the front of his boxers was wide open the whole time.

'He's seen Stuart's winkle!' she shrieks in horror, causing me to snort coffee out my nose.

After reassuring her that he's probably seen much worse on the tour bus, I leave her and head back to my office, still laughing and feeling confident that the £9.64 I'd just spent was definitely a necessity.

Wednesday 24 May – Day 10

I've taken the day off work to go scooter shopping, having decided that the cycling option isn't practical (in other words, I still can't find my cycling shorts).

I've gone through the options of getting a bigger engine but it's too much money and I'd need to start sitting tests, which would just add to the expense. Cheap and cheerful is the key here and that means 50 cc.

After running Hobbs round the park, I head to the motorbike shop. Despite my best efforts, I can't find any excuse to go back to Rome and buy the scooter there, so have to settle for a dealership in the leafy suburbs of Glasgow's south side. I've already looked at the available scooters on the internet and have no reason to doubt that the cheapest one is perfect for me.

Before Shopping Ban (BSB) I would have arrived at the shop and convinced myself that the dearest one was best. I'd then spend three hours torturing myself with all of the pros and cons before making a decision that felt horribly wrong a week later.

But I can't do that anymore. I force myself to make the cheapest choice and then take the advice of the sales staff about the other things I need, so I can get the whole lot within my budget.

For once, I feel confident with my purchases, mainly because I listened to them rather than the voice in my head that used tell me to take the most expensive option.

I whizz home (30 miles an hour, going downhill, with the wind behind me) and call my parents to tell them their daughter is almost a Hell's Angel.

My mother says it's the most sensible thing I've ever done and that she's proud of me. Suddenly I'm six again and coming home with a prize from school.

> £ Scooter splurge – £1,727.08

(And this is me supposed to be saving money?!)

Thursday 25 May – Day 11

I am officially Scooter Girl! My motorbike helmet seems so huge that I look like a travelling mushroom, but I don't care.

My colleagues love my little machine and I nip in and out of work without any problems, feeling extremely pleased with myself, if a little wobbly at the traffic lights.

Best of all, other bikers and scooter riders wave to you as you go by. I feel like I've become a member of a club that I didn't even know existed.

When I get home, I go through my wages, pay my bills and work out how much extra I have from the overtime I've done. After working out the money I need for food and necessities for the rest of the month, I have around £200 to spare.

I pick up the phone and transfer it straight to my credit card.

Instead of mourning the loss of the fabulous shoes it could have bought me, I feel elated. Can I really be getting into this experiment so soon? Or is this merely the honeymoon period?

Friday 26 May – Day 12

I've been offered the chance to work the public holiday and earn myself some extra money.

I'd love to just have a long lie-in and a day off with Kevin, but I can do that at the weekend. Kevin agrees, but backs off and leaves me to make the right choice.

I think of my debt, don my crash helmet and arrive at my desk for 8 am.

Saturday 27 May – Day 13

After feeling so assured and confident that I could handle the year ahead, I almost lose it today when I check out my emails.

Johnnie Boden is stalking me!

There he is, inviting me to check out this season's fabulous 'flippy' skirt and appropriately mismatched velvet-trimmed cardigan and all with free postage and packing. It's all I need to see me through the summer.

My fingers flutter over the keyboard, my head filled with images of me on a beach in a floppy hat ... then I come to my senses and find the strength to hit the delete button.

Hobbs gets dragged out for a two-hour walk, while I cool off from my moment of near-madness.

I'm torn between being annoyed with myself for nearly giving in so soon and being annoyed that though I worked yesterday I still can't treat myself.

Part of my problem seems to be that I feel I have to be rewarded for everything I do.

Just two days ago, I was delighted to put my extra pounds towards my debt, feeing like I'd taken a step forward and now I'm behaving like a spoilt child, stomping around and trying not to cry because I can't go shopping.

Sunday 28 May – Day 14

It gets worse!!

Today I log on and there's an invite to the LK Bennett fashion evening. I adore their totally impractical kitten heels in the palest pastel suede, so soft you'd swear they were actually made from real kittens.

It feels like I'm being tortured and tested all at once. I probably got these kind of invites all the time, but didn't take so much notice BSB, because I had the choice of going.

I delete it immediately and rush to the kitchen to find solace in a jar of Nutella.

Kevin says nothing. He knows that I'm on a short fuse and even encouraging words would feel patronising right now. Instead he sneaks surreptitious looks over the top of his newspaper, attempting to draw me into conversation via interesting little articles that he's reading.

I notice he avoids any topic relating to the financial pages.

Monday 29 May – Day 15

My email is being kinder to me today and even provides me with a laugh-out-loud moment courtesy of my oldest friend Kate.

Every since we were small, she wanted more than anything else to be a mother, so when she suffered a miscarriage, it was a heavy blow.

The second was harder to take and the third left Kate and her husband Simon wondering if they would ever be parents.

But miracles do happen and when Emma did finally make her grand entrance to the world, Simon even said that he recognised her as the little person they were meant to have all along. That still makes me cry.

As none of us are hugely religious, godparents didn't seem terribly appropriate. Instead I was asked if I would be Emma's fairy godmother. How could I turn that down?! Who wouldn't want to make a little girl's wishes come true?

Anyway, today Kate has sent me a photograph of the French au pair that she's agreed to house for six months. The original idea was to provide the eighteen-year-old with a great place to live and the chance to brush up on her English, then Kate saw her picture …

The girl is beyond beautiful with long, honey-coloured hair and a glowing, peachy tan!

After much careful consideration, Kate feels the best idea is to feed her pies and chips, refuse to let her out in daylight and tell her that the bowl cut is the latest London hair trend.

Tuesday 30 May – Day 16
The post arrives with the loveliest surprise!

My stepdad sent a cheque for £100 to go towards paying off my scooter.

Wednesday 31 May – Day 17
I meet my best friend Kirsty for a three-hour dinner in our favourite restaurant. I say it's our favourite restaurant, but it's possibly the only place in Scotland that would tolerate our lengthy stay and goose-honk laughter between courses.

We also flirt outrageously with the waiter – mainly because we can, but also because he's a captive audience and can't run away very easily. We flatter ourselves by pretending he stays because he likes it.

I scooter over and park in the same space as Kirsty's dinky little car. We stand outside for a few moments, squeaking about how cute it all is and how terribly continental I am with my helmet on one arm and my Mulberry trout bag on the other.

Kirsty is one of the few people to know the true extent of my shopping habit, and as a result feels genuinely sorry for me and worried that I'll manage to last through the year ahead.

We talk about a party that I'm supposed to be going to next month and my impending dilemma at not being able to buy anything new to wear to it. She suggests that if I'm stuck for an outfit, I'm welcome to rifle through her wardrobes and borrow something fab.

As I know how precious she is about her clothes, this is a huge gesture and – although I already know it – confirms just what a good friend she is.

We finally leave and tip the waiter for putting up with us (his poor face must be killing him from all that smiling) and as we walk out the door, all my continental charm disappears.

It's pouring and I end up standing at the side of the road, hopping on one foot while trying to get the other into the leg of my waterproofs. You wouldn't see that in the Piazza del Popolo.

I ride home coveting Kirsty's car.

2

Never have I wanted to shop more!

June 2006

Debt to date = £32,375.46

Thursday 1 June – Day 18

Oh, the sheer indulgence of buying something other than food.

I bought a thank-you card for my stepdad for his generous contribution to my new mode of transport, then picked up the Father's Day cards I needed while I was there.

I have to buy three Father's Day cards – that's one for my stepdad from me, one for my stepdad from Hobbs (which has to say Grandpa on the front) and one for Kevin* from Hobbs.

A task that would normally have taken five minutes took me over half an hour as I savoured the purchasing process, browsing through every row of cards until I found the most fitting ones.

They may just be cards, but they've given me a little hit of the retail therapy that I've been craving.

---

*Although neither of us will ever admit it to the other, Kevin and I get quite upset if we don't get cards from the dog on Father's Day, Mother's Day, birthdays and Christmas.

Friday 2 June – Day 19

What's wrong with me?! I've turned into a stroppy cow, who's had a run-in with one of her colleagues.

Secretly, I think I've been hankering after an argument for the past week. Subconsciously or otherwise, perhaps I engineered my office outburst slightly to give myself the excuse for a much needed blowout.

But instead of even thinking about apologising, my mind is filled with thoughts of how I could relieve the stress with a quick spot of shopping.

When I do finally escape the atmos of the office, I feel even more trapped by the fact that I can't cheer myself up with a pair of spangly flip-flops or a feel-good fragrance.

Feeling desperately sorry for myself, I skulk back to the office with my lousy lunch deal and clock-watch until home time.

Saturday 3 June – Day 20

My mood hasn't improved since my workplace wobbly and my previous high and cocky confidence has been replaced with complete despair and self-doubt.

I've spent almost 48 hours sulking and making Kevin's life a misery, because obviously it's his fault that I'm in this situation.

A trip to the shopping centre doesn't exactly send my spirits soaring – it's huge, soulless and full of things that I can't buy. Never have I wanted to shop more!

My petted lip is like a sink, as I drag myself around the shops whinging. It isn't long before Kevin can't take any more of my bad-tempered toddler behaviour and we head back to the car. Even as we're leaving, I'm still desperately looking for something I can justify buying and almost cave in and buy a watch. It would have brought my collection of timepieces up to eight and if I'm honest, it was only Kevin's intervention (dragging me by the hand) that stopped me.

When we get home, we take Hobbs for a long walk in the sunshine and although it doesn't totally lift my mood, it helps me to see that another watch wouldn't really have made me feel good about myself. In fact, I'd have been furious with myself for having blown the experiment so early on.

It's only when we're relaxing later in the evening and I really think about it, that it hits me that I've felt like this before.

When I stopped smoking! I managed that with nicotine patches – shame there isn't a shopping version.

Sunday 4 June – Day 21

I always write a 'To Do' list at the start of the week, usually by just updating the saved document on the computer and printing it off.

Quite why I bother, I don't know. The second the sheet is off the printer, I've forgotten all about the list and every item on it. I usually find it a month later covered in coffee-cup rings with not a single item ticked off or completed.

Today I decide to lug out some of the A4 pads that I seem to have been amassing* in case of some global paper crisis and write the list by hand.

It takes me ages and my wrist is aching by the time I finish. No wonder I go through so many printer cartridges; the list is two pages long!

Two things learned today – I rely on the keyboard too much and I have too many things on that damn list.

*Since I was a child, I have had an obsession with notepads and pens. When other kids were asking for dolls, I was begging my parents to buy me another pen set and groovy multicoloured pad. My mother has only recently revealed how weird she thought I was.

Monday 5 June – Day 22

Kevin has been off work sick today.

When I'm off sick, I lie on the couch making pathetic noises, putting the consumption-ridden heroines of Victorian novels to shame.

Kevin, however, has managed to drag himself from his deathbed to indulge in bit of light dusting and tidying. Where piles of magazines, ironing and various other items that were no longer loved or required used to reside, I see all of the lovely pieces that we've sourced so carefully and bought with such excitement.

For the first time in ages, the living room feels like a room I want to live in, rather than where I perch on the edge of my seat, fretting and fussing about the mess and clutter, but doing nothing about it.

If nothing else, this week is definitely teaching me that less is more.

Tuesday 6 June – Day 23

After two weeks of town travel, the petrol gauge on the scooter was hovering near the empty mark. So, this morning, I stopped to fill up on my way to work.

I'd barely squeezed the nozzle when it started doing that weird clunking thing that indicates the tank is full.

I wiggle the nozzle about and squeeze again. Clunk!

I grab the scooter and shake it a bit, then squeeze again. Clunk! (I love when you see people rocking their cars with their bums, tongues between teeth, concentrating on squeezing that last drop into the tank.)

I look at the petrol pump with my mind still in car-driver mode, thinking there must be something wrong when I see £2.92 on the dial.

I peer into the tank and see the petrol shimmering at the surface. It's full! £2.92 and it's full!

I almost kneel down and kiss the forecourt.

Wednesday 7 June – Day 24

I've run out of eye make-up remover.

Normally this wouldn't pose a problem. I would just trot along to the Chanel counter, pick up another bottle and charge it to my credit card.

Admittedly it would be a miracle of the bottle made it home alone, unaccompanied by a couple of eye shadows, nail varnishes and a lush mascara. But now it's different …

I spied a body lotion in the bathroom as I was getting ready for bed this evening and figuring that one lotion must be pretty much like another, decided to try that out on my lids and lashes.

If you're going to try this yourself, please note: it does work, but for God's sake don't open your eyes to see just how well it's working.

I did and I'm currently writing this with eyes that wouldn't look out of place on that monk in *The Da Vinci Code*.

Thursday 8 June – Day 25

For the first time in their life, my Prada loafers made it out of the box, onto my feet and into work.

I'd put them on to cheer up one of my colleagues, who is as sadly fashion obsessed as me and had been having a bad week.

One of the excuses I use not to wear the loafers is that they're made predominantly of cream fabric. Cream fabric doesn't always fare well in British weather, but today I decided to take the chance. Wearing them on the scooter is a step too far though, so they remain in their shoe bag until I reach the safety of the office carpet.

All was going well until I nipped out to see someone's motorbike (see, I'm part of the gang now) and accidentally rubbed my left shoe against the stand.

Horror!!! A huge black stripe right across the front!!! I barely manage to stifle the scream and flee back to my desk, where at least I can hide my feet underneath and pretend the 'bad thing' hasn't happened. To make matters worse, the woman I'd worn them for has called in sick!

Anyway, after work we set off to visit my parents, who live on an island off the west coast of Scotland. It only takes a couple of hours to get there and they have a wonderful garden that makes Hobbs a very happy dog. It's full of secret sniff places and hedges to hide behind, so he's more than a little excited when he cottons on to why we're loading our cases into the car.

As he springs and twirls at the end of his lead, he manages to stand on my right shoe, producing a smudge to rival the earlier streak. Resisting the urge to place the soiled shoe swiftly against his furry, little backside, I get into the car and vow to wear my trainers next time.

Friday 9 June – Day 26

It's been baking hot all day.

Kevin hit the golf course just after breakfast and after a rather lazy start, trailing round the garden in my pyjamas while Mum tells me the Latin names of everything in it, I set off to the beach with Hobbs, so he can cool off in the sea.

The breakers are massive and at one point he actually seems to be body surfing – providing much amusement to the two small girls who look like emery boards thanks to the combination of sunscreen and sand.

After Mum's garden, water is Hobbs' favourite thing in the world and he loses all sense when he's around it. At least, that's what I try to explain to the poor woman who's just had him race across her picnic rug. She must be a dog lover though, as I manage to leave the beach unscathed.

We set off to meet Kevin and all walk up the road together: him lugging his golf clubs, me trying to control the dog and stop myself eating the strawberries that we've bought from the fruit farm.

Even by dinner time, it's still roasting, so we move all the food to the table outside and sit gazing out across the water, sipping gin and bitter lemon from tall, chilled glasses.

Days like this make me realise that it isn't all about spending money. I think about my funk last weekend at the shopping centre and feel truly ashamed of myself.

Saturday 10 June – Day 27

I've broken the rules and bought something, but I swear it was a necessity and it wasn't even for me.

Although Hobbs had been lying in the shade a lot yesterday, he'd also been haring around – both on the beach and in the garden – and by the time we went to bed he was still panting and quite upset.

He'd obviously had too much heat and sun, so we had to come up with something that would help him cool off and fast ... And what better way to do that, than in a paddling pool!

It was only £10 and Kevin paid half, so I didn't think it was going to make me call off the whole experiment for cheating.

It took hours to fill the damn thing, but before we were even halfway through, Hobbs climbed in and lay down in the water.

I swear you could see a smile on his furry little lips. Surely that's worth bending the rules for?

 Hobbs' hydrotherapy – £5

Sunday 11 June – Day 28

My credit card bills were in the mail when we arrived home last night, so today I had to face the music and look at them.

Until now, this has involved opening the envelope and holding it open ever so slightly, enabling me to see the minimum amount due without actually revealing the full horror of the outstanding balance.

But the experiment dictates that I can no longer bury my head in the sand and bravely I pull out each statement, unfold it and read it.

Incredibly, it wasn't nearly as painful as I thought it would be, probably because I'd already had to add it all up at the start of this experiment and I'm now trying to be adult about the whole thing.

Apart from the fact that I hadn't spent as much in Rome as I'd thought, the totals feel like a challenge. A chance to see them fall with each month that goes by.

But what has really shocked me is the interest I'm paying. Now all those little percentage signs in the terms and conditions section of my statements suddenly make sense to me. In some cases almost of a quarter of the payment I'm making is completely bypassing my outstanding balance and going straight into my creditors' coffers.

I now realise that I'm going to have to take this into account when I'm working out how much of my debt I'm clearing each month.

These sheets of paper show the true cost of all my indulgences and the reason that I'm having to face my financial monsters.

Although, I'm still hiding them from Kevin.

Monday 12 June – Day 29

My back is agony. I've spent the day walking around like I have a plank stuck down the back of my jacket and a spike shoved up my bottom.

I catch sight of myself in a shop window and think I'm being followed by Max Wall, before realising it's my own reflection.

Even though I have a slight curve in my spine, I'm usually free from aches and pains. Thinking that maybe I need a little posture correction and some more flexibility, I call the local pilates and yoga centre, to see if they can offer a solution.

They can – but the consultation is £46 followed by a block booking of sessions at £150. Ouch! My wallet is more pained than I am.

I think I'm going to have to look for an alternative to the alternative therapy.

Tuesday 13 June – Day 30

I've been worrying about my skincare situation (well, what else is there to worry about when you're thirty-odd grand in debt?)

Having tried too many brands to mention, my skin has settled down for a long and happy relationship with the Chanel Precision range. They're not the priciest products out there, but they're not the cheapest either and I'm not entirely sure how I'll be able to afford or justify replacing any of them when they run out.

I've already decided to forego the eye make-up remover, but can I cope without the rest?

In case of cosmetic emergencies, I've been raking about in drawers and cupboards to see what else I could use and I'm truly horrified.

There are hordes of samples gathered from previous facials or when I've looked sweetly enough at counter assistants for them to chuck a handful in with my purchases. These are now neatly stored in a big glass jar in the bathroom with a 'USE ME' sticker on it.

But they weren't the biggest shocker. Here's what else I found:

> 41 nail varnishes
> 29 shower gels and soaps
> 27 body lotions
> 8 shampoos and their matching conditioners
> 7 deodorants
> 3 unopened face creams

Just how much skin and hair do I think I have?! Tempting though it is to give my make-up the same inventory treatment, I think the toiletries total has served its purpose – flagging up my complete inability to know when I have enough of something.

Wednesday 14 June – Day 31

In my spare time I do PR for a local band and a singer/songwriter and tonight is the band's strategy meeting.

They're just starting out and as they're friends, there's no charge. Besides it's great getting together with them, because they're all so enthusiastic and it doesn't cost me anything other than my time. I get my payment in pride when I see them in the paper or hear their gigs mentioned on the radio.

I scooter into town (free parking, I still can't get over that) and meet them in a bar, where we get our heads together – in true rock-and-roll style – over a sparkling mineral water. We lay out their hopes and dreams for the forthcoming year.

It stretches to two sheets of A4 paper, covered in scribbles that I'll interpret and email to them later. It's only when I get home and start typing it up that it occurs to me – not one of the things on the list has a cost in monetary terms.

(While I feel cool hanging around with the band in my biker-chic gear in the pub, they insist on following me outside to stand in a group and wave to me as I drive away. I hate them! As they are fall about laughing, I pull away from the pavement trying to maintain my dignity on what can only be described as a hairdryer with wheels.)

Thursday 15 June – Day 32

A website I subscribe to is looking for a freelance copywriter and have sent me an email about it. I reply immediately, delighted to have finally found an email that could make me money rather than encourage me to spend it.

I dare say several thousand other people have received the same email, but nothing ventured …

It also reminds me that I'm owed money from a woman I did some website work for over a year ago. Despite numerous calls and reminders, she has, so far, managed to sidestep paying me, coming up with every excuse in the book except for a natural disaster.

I come over all assertive and call her. She always answers by about the third ring, but tonight it rings out before going to voicemail. Undeterred I leave a message on her mobile, then spend the rest of the evening wondering if she may actually have been struck by a plague of locusts.

One can but hope …

Friday 16 June – Day 33

Despite my previous distress at having to be in the vicinity of more than one shop, I brace myself to go into town with Kevin after work.

He isn't in the same financial dire straits as me and can afford to go on a splurge. This hurts me in a way I'd never thought possible.

But there's no point in me trailing miserably in his wake, so I force myself to get excited about the stuff that he's buying and to my absolute amazement it works. I'm getting my fix by proxy!

I start trawling the rails, looking for other things for him to try on. Having packed as many items as I can into the tiny changing room, I then settle down on the sofa outside, rejecting certain looks and rejoicing in others, as he appears from behind the curtain to strut his stuff.

It doesn't take us long to whittle it down to a few key items and laden with bags, we set off for the car. On the way back there's a French market in the square and tempted by the atmosphere and aromas we decide to go for a quick mooch around.

We hit the crepe stall first and blowing on our fingers, nibble down the piping hot treat, each of us pretending to the other that we aren't imagining we're in Paris.

Suddenly my eyes are out on stalks. Two feet in front of me is the bag stall. There are gorgeous, floppy satchels in every possible colour and like passionate Parisians, they're begging me to take them home.

I display some true British reserve, bid them *adieu* and walk away.

Saturday 17 June – Day 34

This whole experiment is about scaling down and, if I'm honest, every area of my life could do with a little paring back.

I'm starting with my clothes.

I enter the bedlam that's our bedroom and tip the contents of every drawer onto the bed, pile the teetering ironing mounds beside them and then start hauling the hangers from the wardrobe.

Even though I have a rough idea of how much clothing I possess, it's still a shock to see it piled that high. It's more of a shock though to admit that I probably don't wear even a quarter of it.

I make four piles: bin, charity, sell and keep. The last is the largest and isn't helped by the fact that I keep rescuing things from the other piles. But it's a start and I'm sure that once I get the hang of this, it'll be easier.

Right now though, it's stressing me out. I desperately want to declutter and feel free of this burden, but at the same time I can't bring myself to part with any of it.

It doesn't help that in the middle of it all Mum phones to say that she has also been having a clear-out and has found a box with my dog collection in it. Basically this is a cardboard box that contains around 30 dog ornaments from my childhood.

Most of them are pottery and as far as I can remember, there are very few with all of the legs that are usually required of a quadruped.

Instead of telling her to bin them, I tell her that we'll pick them up next time we're over. What?!

Then I stupidly ask her if she can see a little dachshund, which is made from leather and used to be my favourite. What a mistake that was! Have you ever heard anyone shuffle pottery?

If any of them had managed to retain four legs, they certainly haven't got them all now.

Sunday 18 June – Day 35

I've just realised that we don't own a digital camera.

So how the hell am I going to sell the clothes I've set aside for eBay?

Describe them well and send prospective buyers a line drawing?!

Monday 19 June – Day 36

Aah, the joy of pay day. But joy is short-lived.

I've had the money in my bank for less than twelve hours and despite doing overtime, I'm already down to less than £200. I know that the scooter purchase has dented my finances a bit, but I was hoping for a little more pocket money this month.

Well, I guess it's just another tricky situation that I'll have to overcome. Take it on the chin. See it as a challenge and all that. Although I admit that I'm gritting my teeth as I write this.

Last month I paid nearly £1,000 towards my debts and managed to get all the way through to today without purging the plastic. I've never done that before.

I usually make it until the week prior to pay day, before admitting defeat and raiding my credit cards for a couple of hundred pounds to see me through.

It's hard to kick a habit like that and today I was all fired up, ready to shop as soon as I saw my wage-slip. Even though my head knew I was only allowed to buy lunch, my heart was soaring as I walked round the shops. Every little beat quickening at the prospect of the perfect pair of shoes or a chunky, funky watch to set off my summer look.

But this year, my summer, autumn, winter and spring looks will have to be put together from my imagination and existing wardrobe. The changes that I make to my wardrobe for each season can't be bought anymore; they have to be adapted.

This mightn't seem too alarming right now, but there are 329 days left to this experiment and the level of my temptation today makes me think that could be 328 days too many.

Tuesday 20 June – Day 37

I had to get my hair cut today – when you start to look like a Shetland pony then it falls into the necessity category.

I've been meaning to change to a hairdresser near my work, so I can go in during my lunch hour, but the ones in town always seem either too expensive or too scary.

By scary, I mean the kind of place where you have to go in looking as though you've just come off the catwalk. The kind of place where you sit in a chair while they revolve you slowly, making worried noises and pulling faces that suggest you're more in need of serious plastic surgery than a mere trim of your split ends.

But today I found a place five minutes from my office, which I felt certain would induce neither bankruptcy nor a heart attack. They're friendly, they're reasonably priced and they were able to take me this evening.

So, after dinner I scooter back into town and place my tresses at their mercy. Forty-five minutes later, I emerge sleek and groomed with a haircut that actually suits me and – unbelievably – that I'm happy with.

To add to the joy, I discover that in between cuts they'll trim my fringe for free, so although the haircut is slightly more expensive than my usual, the gratis trim balances it out.

Also, I've recently cancelled a direct debit for some useless insurance against ant invasion or some other unlikely eventuality, so the £16.50 I've saved each month will more than cover the additional cost.

Kevin rolls his eyes when I return. He likes the cut but can't understand why I had to change my hairdresser in the first place.

I point out that six months ago he changed his barber for one that charged £4 extra, but provided a 'free' beer while he waited. Silence …

£ **Shampoo and shear – £32**

Wednesday 21 June – Day 39

Oh my God! I have neck spots!

How do you get neck spots? No idea? Then I'll tell you.

In a bid to eke out my beloved Chanel skincare, I decided to utilise the many other tubs and samples that I'd found recently. So, every morning and night, I've been slathering them on my neck and, hey presto, I have neck spots!

I've now remembered why I stopped using those creams in the first place.

This has reinforced two things that I already suspected.

1. I have sensitive skin.
2. I'm going to have to save up if I want to stick with my preferred brand.

To add insult to injury, I've heard nothing back from the website that was looking for a freelance copywriter (despite two emails) and the woman who has owed me money for over a year is still studiously ignoring me.

I have a horrible feeling that I'm going to have to write that one off and treat it as a lesson learned.

(Incidentally, I haven't thrown the creams in the bin – I can't afford to. I'm just hoping that my legs don't develop the same horny-toad look as my neck!)

Thursday 22 June – Day 40

My bad-back days may be behind me, so to speak.

I was chatting to one of my colleagues today and apparently we have a physiotherapist at our work. It's amazing the things you find lurking around in the back of a cupboard!

She gave me her number and although I was expecting a barrage of questions followed by a 'Sorry, we can't help you', she says she'll call me back with an appointment over the next couple of weeks.

I'm so happy! This sounds a lot better than a batch of painkillers and infinitely better than having to spend all that money on the yoga consultation and subsequent classes that I looked at recently.

BSB, I wouldn't have thought twice about signing up for those sessions. I'd have justified it to myself and then worried about how to pay for it later, all the time telling myself that because it was expensive, it must be good.

Perhaps when I don't just leap at the first thing I see, I can find a cheaper – and possibly better – solution.

Friday 23 June – Day 41

Kevin has finally sold one of the cars, meaning I can cancel the insurance I have for it and save myself some more money.

Apparently though I have to pay a cancellation fee of £45, then they work out the number of months I have left, divide it by 40, multiply it by 29, subtract two, run it past Pythagoras and I get what's left over.

I look forward to my £0.40 cheque.

Saturday 24 June – Day 42

To say I feel rough today is like saying that Jimmy Choo makes 'not bad' shoes.

Last night, we had an Italian night and invited our friends, Chris and Matt, over. I used to go to school with Matt and Chris is his older brother.

They live just a few streets away from us and if we're lucky we'll see them a handful of times a year, but when we do, we really make up for it and last night was no exception.

We played host instead of going to a restaurant (another economising move) and although I say so myself, I made a pretty good job of the grub. I'm assuming the others agree, as neither has called yet to say I owe them for the supply of Pepto-Bismol they've had to buy.

We laughed, chatted, nibbled and worked our way through most of the bottles of fizz we had in the fridge, before kicking back with some duty-free limoncello and a cigar each.

The irony being that none of us usually smoke and constantly seek out places where we won't get puffed on. We welcomed the Scotland-wide smoking ban with open arms and yet, there we were, happily sitting around in a haze, choking and spluttering and enjoying every second of it.

Poor Hobbs, even he looks like he's had a heavy evening and spends his Saturday afternoon snoozing off his hangdog hangover with the rest of us.

Sunday 25 June – Day 43

My neck pustules may have subsided but the rest of my skin is a mess.

Too many nights of falling asleep with my make-up on are taking their toll on my face.

What doesn't help is my determination to sneak in some of those opened skincare products that were bought with such promise in store: newer, fresher skin in just the swipe of a toner; a complexion plumped, youthful and dewy with the application of the latest miracle moisturiser.

With such a variety of cosmetics in use, my skin's crying out for some restoration of normality and just one set of products.

BSB I would have picked up the phone, called the beautician and booked myself in for a facial, but now I can't justify the expense.

My alternative is to get out the steam iron and stand with my head drooped over the ironing board while I smooth out those creases (on the linen, not my face). It may not be quite the same as the steam I enjoy at the salon – snuggled up under a blanket listening to whale music – but it helps to make me feel a little better and I get the extra pleasure of slipping into my bed later with a set of cool, crisp, freshly ironed sheets. Bliss!

Monday 26 June – Day 44

I'm working late today, so instead of nipping out for food, I opt to take in some dinner. Generally, this involves a three-minute dash around the grocery section of the garage where I stop for petrol.

Three minutes in the place is my limit. This is because I'm either already late for work or because I've spotted a jar of Nutella that propels me into a dreamlike state. I imagine all the fun I'll have eating it, then have to listen to my 'you'll only get fat' conscience before legging it to the counter with my prize, fingers in ears, shouting: 'I can't hear you!'

So there I am shuffling round the mini aisles – trying to avoid the one where I know the Nutella resides – and putting a few choice items in my basket including a frozen curry dinner for one (oh the dizzy heights of fine dining).

When I get to the till they discover that the bar code on the curry won't register, so while I'm looking around for a chair to sit out the next half-hour that it will no doubt take to involve the manager and the subsequent reassessing of the entire store's pricing system – the guy at the checkout decides that he can't be bothered with the hassle and gives me the dinner for free!

I make an Olympic dash to the scooter before he changes his mind.

I've had this particular dish a thousand times before, but it's amazing how much better it tastes tonight.

Tuesday 27 June – Day 45

I meet Kate for lunch today. She's up from London, visiting the in-laws and has left her petite and perfect offspring with them while we get together for an hour.

To save some time, she meets me at work and we head to the canteen to see how close we can get to the school dinners of old. We excel ourselves with fish and chips, followed by the most gelatinous trifle we've ever stood a spoon in.

It's great to see her and hear her news. One of the other reasons for her trip north of the border is that she's taking part in a hill walk through the weekend to raise money for a cancer charity.

It's a subject close to our hearts. Kate and I both lost our fathers to the illness and Kevin's mum is currently fighting it like a demon.

I donate all I can afford at the moment to the cause, wishing it was more and realising that if I wasn't so deep in debt, it could be.

£ Spartan sponsorship – £20

Wednesday June 28th – Day 46

Okay, I take back everything bad I've ever said about insurance companies.

This morning they sent me the usual 'sorry to have lost your business' letter and to tell me they were reimbursing me to the tune of £59.

I can't believe it! I even read the letter twice, thinking that was what they were charging me for cancelling on them. Thankfully, there'll be no temptation on my part to spend it, as they're paying it straight back into my credit card.

When I arrive at work, I find that our computer system was still in the same condition as when I'd clocked in on Monday – not working.

I spend another eight-hour shift shuffling piles of useless paperwork from one end of my desk to the other. Useless, because the rest of the information that I need to get working on my projects is currently trapped in cyberspace.

Thursday 29 June – Day 47

I had my appointment with the work's physiotherapist today and it was fantastic.

Instead of being laughed out of the curtained cubicle, I got the most incredibly thorough questioning before being asked to perform a set of random, bizarre movements.

This wasn't, as I suspected, an attempt to set me up on some hidden camera show and apparently my moves made sense to her. She patiently explained to me what she could feel and see with the assistance of a plastic spine, like the ones you used to see hanging in the science-room cupboard at school that gave you a heart attack if you accidentally touched it when the lights were off.

Then she talked me through a set of exercises to do twice a day. If she's happy with my progress in a few weeks' time, then I don't even need to see her again.

It's the best advice and help that I've had for my back and I'm astounded that I got it without having to pay for it.

Friday 30 June – Day 48

The IT department have finally got our system up and running. (Apparently they just switched it off, then switched it back on again.)

I never thought I'd say it but it's a relief to be able to get some work done and I rattle through as much as I can before caving in and replying to the emails sent by my friends.

Today was also the day that I got to see the corporate video I had taken part in. The idea was for me to interview my boss, discussing topics that affect us all at work and addressing issues that may come up in the future.

Unfortunately some of my colleagues had seen it before me and a few emailed their comments on my performance. Most were highly complimentary (not!), but my favourite came in the form of a phone call.

Charmer: 'Didn't realise you had an older, fatter sister.'

Me: 'Thanks for that – didn't my hair look nice and shiny though?'

Charmer: 'Yeah I suppose so, did you iron it?'

Me: 'Well, kind of. I straightened it.'

Charmer: 'Shame you never thought to iron your face then.'

Oh ha ha! My sides are splitting. Shame I can't max out my credit card with a dose of Botox. I can still hear his hysterical laughter at the other end of the phone as I hang up.

3

I swear it was an accident ...

July 2006

Debt to date = £31,624.16

Sunday 2 July – Day 50

We're back from another blissful weekend at our country bolt-hole, otherwise known as my parent's house. Hobbs is shattered from two days of non-stop playing and launching himself into his paddling pool, Kevin's tan looks deeper and I'm pink and itchy from too much sun. But we're all happy and relaxed.

I did notice something rather revealing about myself this weekend. When I'm in the city I'm ultra conscious of the way I look: the labels I wear, the bag I carry and the many expensive products that I'm compelled to slather on my skin and hair.

When I'm in the country all of that goes out the window!

I'm not saying that I go around dressed in rags with a bird's nest of hair plastered onto my head, but I'm quite happy to use the cheapest of products. Supermarket own-brand shampoos and toothpaste are perfectly acceptable to my 'country girl' persona but I wouldn't dream of using them back home in the city.

Why not? Why are lesser labels only okay for me to use some of the time? Do I honestly think that the brand police are going to come to my house and go through the contents of my bathroom cabinet? Will my workmates know by my smile that I've used a non-designer dental wash? Hardly! It's time I got more in tune with my less snobbish side and started saving on the basics.

Monday 3 July – Day 51

Well, I made it this far and blew it!

I bought a magazine. I swear it was an accident – a moment of habit, nothing more – and I didn't even realise I'd done it until I got back to the office and emptied my bag out. There it was, lurking at the bottom, sniggering at the look of horror on my face when I spotted it in all its glossy glory.

I know, I know … How is it possible to 'accidentally' buy a magazine? Well, I'll tell you, it's a damn sight easier than I thought!

I'd been having a smug 'look at me not buying shoes' moment during my break, wandering round the shops picking up healthy nibbles for lunch without a thought in my head other than what kind of apples to get and without even realising it, I must have just chucked the mag in the basket.

I didn't even notice at the checkout because I was so busy eyeing up the chocolate display in front of the till. Incidentally, why do shops do that? It's beyond cruel to anyone who has just spent the best part of their day reading the calorie content on every item in the store, to then push them over the edge by making them queue in front of all of those glistening wrappers. Thankfully, at least I managed not to cave on

this front. The thought of the magazine *and* a cheaty chocolate bar could have been enough to make me quit the whole
experiment.

Although I'm angry with myself, I'm grateful it was a
cheapy publication and not one of those fabulous biannual
things that cost a week's wages. Anyway, it's taught me that
feeling smug is all very well as long as I'm aware that some
habits are not only hard to break, they've also developed into
involuntary actions.

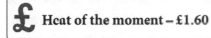

£ Heat of the moment – £1.60

Tuesday 4 July – Day 52

Another day, another purchase, but today it was legit and it
felt great!

Last night when I was filling up our little whistling kettle,
I noticed something in the bottom of it. Closer inspection
revealed rust which sent me into a fit of panic, followed by
three hours of stressing about all of the horrible diseases we
might have subjected ourselves to by drinking rusty, boiled
water. I'm sure there aren't any, but there's nothing like a
burst of hypochondria to spur you into action.

We trawled the internet for the best – and cheapest – stove-
top kettle. The choice was endless, but we kept coming back
to the glorious Le Creuset ones that perch so satisfyingly on
top of the cooker, like a kettle version of those old-fashioned
nannies with the uniform and formidable bosom.

Kevin's colour choice leans towards granite, I'm smitten with the red, but we both see the sense in browsing first to see what other options are available.

So today, armed with the help and advice of my esteemed shopping colleague, Alison, we set off for the nearest kitchenware store that we can reach during our lunch hour.

Fifteen minutes later, we're surrounded by a plethora of pots and pans, then … my eye is caught by the gleaming glory of that enamelled body and there it sits – the King of Kettles.

I look at the price (£50), fondle its glistening curves, look at the price again (still £50) and then spy an adorable cream, retro-looking little thing that boasts a £24.95 price tag. Without hesitation, I pick up the box and go to the till.

As the money was coming from the joint account that pays for all of our household needs, I didn't even have to feel guilty about spending that £50, but something made me stop and question it. Am I really changing or am I just still reeling from yesterday's magazine mistake?

I don't know the answer, but I do know that Kevin and I have a shiny new kettle that we both love and I swear it boils the water faster than our last one.

Wednesday 5 July – Day 52

The weather's been amazing today and has given me much to think about in the way of natty little summer outfits. Mostly I've been thinking that I have none and can buy none.

But I refuse to let it get me down. What's the point? There's nothing I can do about it until next year and in any case, with my luck I'd purchase an entire wardrobe of light, crisp, perfect pieces that would remain on the hanger because

I was either a) feeling too fat to wear them, b) worrying that I wasn't tanned enough for them, or c) back to living in my wellies and jeans because the weather had turned to tropical storm.

You see – it never rains but it pours!

Thursday 6 July – Day 53

Having managed to avoid most of the emails tempting me into forbidden purchases, I find myself ogling the Charles Tyrwhitt sale catalogue that slipped through the letterbox this morning. Never have so many candy-striped shirts looked so sweet.

Of course, this would be the time that Kevin decides he needs a quick restock, claiming that two of his shirts look a little frayed (rather like my temper when I can't buy something).

He glances through the pages, while I sit opposite pre-tending not to be bothered by the impending purchase I'm sensing. I'm plunged deeper into despair when he logs on to the website and selects two heavenly garments for the bargain price of £75.

I know it's beneath me and please believe me when I say that I couldn't help it, but I actually begged him to buy me a shirt. I pouted, wheedled and whined in an effort to convince him that it would be of benefit to round it up to an even hundred pounds. Obviously this is purely for his own sake, as it would be an easier number for him to deduct from his bank balance.

Buy my efforts are in vain. He point blank refuses and I go into a hefty sulk. I'm losing my touch if I can't even persuade him to cheat on my behalf!

Friday 7 July – Day 54

I'd arranged to meet Verity for a coffee at lunchtime today and spent the entire time fidgeting because my suit was too tight. I felt so uncomfortable and so conscious of the straining fabric and buttons, that I could hardly relax. Scootering to work may well be quicker and more economical, but it means that I'm missing out on at least 40 minutes of extra walking every day.

Even after my clear-out, my wardrobe is still bursting with clothes that are half a stone too tight. I could have a whole new image, that wouldn't cost me a single penny, if I could only get into some of that stuff.

It's clear that shopping's not my only problem. What I seem to be looking at here is an excess-all-areas lifestyle, that's shattered my credit rating and made my thighs rather over friendly with one another.

If I can take my shopping in hand, then maybe I can start on some other parts of my life that also need a little pruning. After all, they say it's easier to give up smoking and drinking at the same time, because you can't decide which loss is more painful.

Saturday 8 July – Day 55

My scooter got its six-week service today. Thankfully it was free. I hadn't bargained for the normal six-month service to hit the £100 mark, so it's just as well I'm saving so much on petrol. Despite using it every day, so far I've only put fuel in three times and the most it's cost me is £2.92.

Kevin's shirts arrived from Tyrwhitt's today. I felt so horribly consumed with jealousy as he unwrapped them – lifting them from their box and sliding them lovingly from their cellophane wrapper. In my unreasonable state, it was like watching him undressing a lover.

The situation was made far worse by the fact that they're gorgeous and he looks fantastic in them.

Sunday 9 July – Day 56

T in the Park is on this weekend and sold out in record time, because Glastonbury's having a well-earned rest this year. Sadly, we had neither the money nor the time to go and queue for tickets, so we're having to rely on the television for our festival fix. But somehow the atmos just isn't right …

We flick the lights on and off, dim them, put them back up on full again, pretend we're there by closing our eyes and swaying with our hands in the air, but it's no use. The only way to really get that festival feeling, is to go camping.

After much rummaging we find the tent, get the camping lantern out and set the whole lot up in our front room. Fantastic! We sit in the little doorway with a perfect view of the stage. It's not raining and we won't have to stand in a mile-long line waiting for the loo. We have an onsite private toilet, hot food facilities and can happily go from band to band without having to trek across a muddy field.

All in all the ideal way to go to a music festival – as long as the neighbours can't see in.

Monday 10 July – Day 56

I'm exhausted! In my bid to be a bit slimmer and fitter, I've just dragged the poor dog out for an hour and a quarter's worth of power walking. It also seemed the ideal way to tire him out but he's still bouncing around, while I wilt like a piece of old lettuce.

I've started to notice a few subtle changes in my attitude just recently. BSB, I would rush home, drag Hobbs out for a quick walk and a chase of his frisbee (him, not me), then get back home to either trawl the internet (for stuff to buy), spend hours scanning mags (for stuff to buy) or just head to the shops themselves (for stuff to buy), mindless with panic that the item I couldn't live without wouldn't be there when I arrived.

Now I'm beginning to realise that if I plan my home time a little better, I can get so many more things done – and actually enjoy doing them instead of seeing them as a chore designed to keep me from my retail therapy.

Tuesday 11 July – Day 57

There are 96 items in the ironing pile. I know this because I counted every single one and because I'll probably have to iron every single one.

What worries me is that that's just the ironing. How many more items are in the wardrobes, drawers and neatly stacked piles that threaten to topple from the chest of drawers and suffocate us in our bed?

I'm quite sure that 96 pieces of clothing (excluding undies and socks) are the norm for most people to have in their entire wardrobe. It makes me stop and wonder just how much money I've invested in that pile and it's not a pleasant thought.

Wednesday 12 July – Day 58
I've got that junk-food face look – you know the one, where you look all bloaty and tired.

It's annoying really because I thought I was being good with my food, but the lack of any visible weight loss and the fact that my face looks like it may erupt into a spot outbreak to rival the moon's surface, tells me I'm kidding myself on. It doesn't matter how you disguise it, chocolate cake can't be classed as health food.

The best solution is salad and fruit and thankfully there's a Boots near to work where I can pick up both as part of a meal deal. I've also found an old advantage card in my wallet that hasn't been taken advantage of quite enough recently. It's time to put it to the test.

I discover that I can get my lunch there for less than £3 and the points I earn can go towards the toiletries that I believe I can't do without. I feel like I'm really getting the hang of this now.

I'll be knitting my own knickers next!

Friday 14 July – Day 60
Apparently there's no such thing as a free lunch, but it seems there is such a thing as a free haircut. Well, kind of ...

Today I went back to the new hairdresser I'd been so pleased with and asked for the fringe trim I'd had been promised free of charge. Now I've fallen for that one before, rocking up at the salon only to discover that to qualify for the free trim between cuts there had to be a 'z' in the month and you had to have less than five hairs in your fringe.

But my faith has been restored. Not only did the girl remember me, greet me like a friend and then pick up the conversation we'd had on the first appointment, but she trimmed my fringe (perfectly) and didn't charge me a penny.

Saturday 15 July – Day 61
I've been very astute this weekend and made myself a little money.

Ages ago I bought a watch that would change my life. It was the answer to all my time-keeping problems and how I'd managed prior to its purchase was a miracle.

Today I found it at the bottom of a drawer, still in its box.

Like too many of my belongings, it had been worn a handful of times and then forgotten about.

Then I remembered that Matt had admired it and even asked me to get one for him, but by the time I'd gone back, the shop no longer had that model.

This is typical of me, leaving things until it's too late and at the time I felt really guilty that I'd let Matt down. Here was a solution and a way to make it up to him, so I called him up and offered him my watch at half price.

He jumped at the chance and by this morning, I had some unexpected funds to put towards my credit card bill.

Monday 17 July – Day 63
We're sunburnt, grubby and covered in insect bites – the result of a weekend camping holiday.

We hadn't planned to go, but the weather was so amazing that it seemed ridiculous not to take advantage of it. So we chucked the tent into the car with all the other knick-knacks that you need for a night under the stars and drove out to the country.

It really couldn't have been more perfect. The campsite was the quietest we'd ever stayed on and we spent the evening lying on the picnic blanket reading the Sunday papers and smoking cigars, while Hobbs curled up to sleep off his day's adventures.

It cost us hardly anything to get away this weekend and once again brings home to me the message that money isn't everything. It didn't stop me coveting our campsite neighbour's split-screen camper van though.

Tuesday 18 July – Day 64

Back to work, but at least it's a short week and even better, it's pay day again.

I have a quick squint through my credit card bills and break my unwritten rule to always pay more than the minimum amount due. I'm on holiday at the end of the month and I want as much cash in the bank as possible, so there's no risk of me raiding my flexible friends.

I do feel a little twinge of conscience as I pay my dues to the exact penny, but how much worse would I feel if I raided my credit cards at this stage?

In the past few years, I've paid them up only to rob them senseless two days before going away. I'd then spend the rest of the year trying to get the balance back down.

This year, what goes down, has to stay down. I'm the financial equivalent of a recovering bulimic.

Wednesday 19 July – Day 65

I may have been in control yesterday but the extra money in my bank account is lurking in the back of my mind. My little shopping Satan is telling me to blow the budget and enjoy my holiday with a few new treats to make it special.

It'd be so easy to do just that and ditch this experiment, but to be honest I feel guilty just thinking about it – as though contemplating cheating on my partner.

I do have an excuse to shop though. We'll be meeting two of my best friends during our holiday and on both occasions it'll be on their birthdays.

Luckily for me, the gifts I've decided on for them are from Clarins, so I'm saved the torment of having to flit from counter to counter while trying my hardest not to collect a 'little something' for myself along the way.

I choose exactly what I have in mind and ask the woman to gift-wrap them, so there's no chance of me hijacking them for myself. I get chatting to her as she wraps and tell her how great my boyfriend's skin is since he stuck to their male grooming range. At that, she smiles, tells me how nice it is to chat and offers me a free sample.

I'm practically doing cartwheels as she rummages about in the drawer before appearing with … a shaving-cream sample for the boyf! I squeak a 'thank you' and walk from the shop, swinging my parcels and biting my lip into a bloody pulp to stop myself crying at the sheer injustice of it all.

Thursday 20 July – Day 66

I've been sent on the most boring training course in history.

Initially I welcomed it as a day away from the office, but after six minutes of listening and three of doodling, I was wishing I was back behind my desk.

I should have known it was going to be bad when the handout was so large it came in a box file.

An hour in, and my eyes start to do that horrible rolling in their sockets thing that happens when you're desperately trying to stay awake and failing miserably.

Thankfully we break for lunch before I totally embarrass myself by falling asleep, which is never easy to disguise when you're sitting in the front row. I'm thinking of how to escape the afternoon session when I'm handed a voucher and told that our two-course lunch in the restaurant is free as part of the course.

Every cloud, as they say …

Friday 21 July – Day 67

I used my last glug of mouthwash this morning and considered the need to buy more while I swished it round my teeth. It took me those few moments to decide that it definitely falls under the necessity category.

I'm heavily into Italian food – a stone and a half too heavily, frankly – and with its high content of garlic and parmesan, I feel I have to consider my colleagues and my love life.

With only their best interests at heart, I opt to purchase the mouthwash.

Sunday 23 July – Day 69

We had our best friends, Kirsty and Davie, over last night and how relieved am I that I replaced the mouthwash?

The evening started off a little more rushed than I'd expected, mainly because I'd forgotten to buy half of the stuff we needed for the meal and was still scootering around the city an hour before our chums were due to arrive. But it all fell into place and I even managed to cook and present the entire meal myself.

That may not sound like an achievement to you, but I can't cook. My lack of culinary skills means that most meals are accompanied by me screeching like a bat at Kevin because it's going wrong and he has to 'do something' that will make it all alright. Or we have the alternative, where I drink one too many gin and tonics, and as a result all I can do is sit on the floor and cry as the oven cremates whatever creation I've put into it.

With the meal a surprising success, I get into celebratory mood and consume a little too much booze and puff on one too many cigars. Hence this morning's gravely voice, doggy breath and desperate need for that mouthwash I nearly didn't buy.

Monday 24 July – Day 70

I'm getting to a point where I'm starting to run low on things that I would usually have a stockpile of. Today, it was mascara.

I'd have thought that sourcing a cheap mascara – that wasn't tested on animals and didn't make my contact lenses so dry that they weld onto my eyes – was a fairly easy thing to do. How wrong I was.

Part of the problem was that my heart was pining for the brand-new, flying-off-the-shelves wonder that Chanel brought out last week, and I have to admit, that was clouding my judgment a little.

I mooched around Boots with my meal deal in my basket trying to work out what I could get by using my loyalty points, when I spotted the perfect peeper preener sitting quietly beside an offer sign. Almay was a brand that I'd used ages ago, it had never given me a problem and here it was, coming to my rescue. I embraced it like a long-lost friend and chucked it in my basket.

I had exactly £10.33 worth of points on my card. My mascara and lunch came to just one penny less. I think it's fair to say I was rather chuffed with myself.

Tuesday 25 July – Day 71

Compared with driving in the car, you see so much more when you're on a scooter. So, on the way home tonight I was amusing myself by reading the billboards while I waited at the traffic lights, when alongside me a bus pulled up advertising Gap.

I stared at the poster for a shop that I could barely go two days without dropping into – on the off chance that everything in my size had been reduced to £9.99 – and it occurred to me that I had completely forgotten about its existence. How can that be possible when it used to play such a huge role in my life? A shop that made me delay going home to my loved ones after work, in case the coat I had my eye on had been put onto the sale rail.

I'm not saying that some shops don't still prey heavily on my mind (you know who you are V V Rouleaux); they appear in my dreams, reeling me in like the child catcher in *Chitty Chitty Bang Bang* – but others, mercifully, have just disappeared from my radar.

Wednesday 26 July – Day 72

I had to deliver some CDs for the band to the other side of the city today and as the weather was so fantastic, I saved myself the postage and jumped on the scooter to deliver them personally.

The parcel was so heavy that the postal costs would have been more than a full tank of petrol for my trusty little mount and it gave me the excuse to go somewhere different during my lunch break.

There really are only so many times that you can stroll up and down the same streets, resisting the urge to splurge, when there are a multitude of shops tempting you to spend, spend, spend.

Zipping along with my jacket open and my visor up, pretending I was in Rome, was a welcome change. The sun twinkled through the leaves as I drove along the side of the park and provided me with a happy moment that kept me going all afternoon.

Thursday 27 July – Day 73

No matter how hard you try to keep your head down and get on with work, the day before your holiday always feels like the last day of school term when you were allowed to bring in a board game from home.

That's how I've been feeling all day, even though we're on such a tight budget that we're staying at my parents' place for the week.

Being a mannerly pair, Kevin and I have organised to go shopping after work for some bits and pieces as a thank you to my parents for playing hosts.

The purchase is mainly toilet-roll based, as my parents think no one else in the world uses as much as I do. My argument is that there are only two of them and when we visit there are twice as many people and therefore the roll goes down more quickly. Their argument is that I'm doing my level best to flush an entire roll at a time in an effort to blow up their septic tank.

Anyway, after purchasing half a hundredweight of loo roll, we go looking for other items that might tickle their fancy. That was when I got carried away and found myself trailing a beige linen skirt around and trying to sneak it into the trolley. Kevin spotted it and despite the lecture and disappointment in his voice, I march to the till and pay for it.

The minute I get in the car, I regret it. By the time we get home, I hate the bloody thing for making me cave and I'm hating myself even more for being so weak!

The receipt is now paper clipped to the hanger and the offending item will be going back for a refund as soon as I return from holiday.

£ Linen lust – £37

4

A chill! In August!

August 2006

Debt to date = £30,782.02

Tuesday 8 August – Day 86

There are some things in life that you should make the most of and holidays are one of them.

I say this because we've just returned from our week-long break at my parent's house. As one of my mother's favourite sayings is 'Friends are like fish; they go off after three days', you can imagine how things went for the other four.

Apparently as you get older, you get more set in your ways, so staying with your parents when you yourself are an adult seems to result in a little friction.

Rigid schedules that can't be changed even when there's nothing else to be done that day don't make for a relaxing atmosphere, and if escaping that means trailing round a golf course in rain so heavy that people are canoeing round the bunkers, then so be it.

Yes, it also rained from the moment we parked in the drive-way. Our images of sun-soaked evenings drinking Pimms on the lawn were replaced by waterproofs and a trip to the vet for the dog because he got a chill! In August!

On top of all that, we were spending a fortune. Eating out for every meal is never a cheap option and there are only so many times that you can sit in the car eating fish and chips while the windows steam up and your arteries clog, before you feel the need for some decent food.

There was, of course, the option of coming home early, but when you have a week off work, then you'll bloody well enjoy it whether you like it or not. You also have that nagging feeling that the moment you return home, the sun will be splitting the trees and the papers will be reporting the sunniest, most fabulous August on record.

So, we decided to grin, bear it, and set up Holiday Fund 2007 the moment we got home.

Our break also gave me the chance to ditch the posh products and test out the bargain-basement options. Somewhere along the way though the chemicals kicked in, leaving my hair like straw and my face like a pizza; a predicament made worse by the fact that I'm not allowed to go to the beautician, get down on my knees and beg her to fix me. Secretly, part of me was rather pleased to finally kick my country-girl persona into touch – she was getting a tad too smug for my liking.

Aside from all the moaning, I have learned a valuable lesson.

You work a lot of hours to earn your holiday, so do the best you can with the money you have. I've come to find that some things are worth splashing out on after all.

Wednesday 9 August – Day 87

Back to work and for the next six months, I'll be working on shifts in another department of the company.

It means a few late nights and getting some time off during the week, but – and like my own, this is rather a big but – I have to work three weekends out of four.

Crying and throwing yourself on the floor doesn't get the management to change their mind over that one – I know, I've tried it. But one of my friends has pointed out that it gives me less opportunity to spend. It's a fair point but it won't stop me missing my lazy weekend mornings with Kevin and Hobbs.

My magazine plopped through the letterbox this morning accompanied by a letter to let me know that my subscription is coming to an end and it's time for me to renew. Damn! I knew it was wishful thinking that they'd just forget and I'd get free copies for the rest of my life. Despite the teeny amount it would cost me to renew – and it really is teeny – I decide I can't possibly justify it.

Besides, its glossy pages only mesmerise me with all the things that I'm missing and that's just one step short of torture at the moment.

Thursday 10 August – Day 88

In a particularly bold move, I use my day off to return the skirt that nearly caused me to fall off the wagon. I glare at it in resentment as it lies in the passenger seat of the car, begging me to keep it and give it a good, loving home.

Lying in the footwell is a pair of Birkenstocks from the same shop that have lain unloved in the box since I bought them back in April. The joy that filled my heart when I saw the receipt still in the box was indescribable – they're going back from whence they came!

Once in the store, I march straight to the refunds desk and hand over the items, along with their receipts. I'm bracing myself for the Birkies getting thrown back in my face for my sheer audacity in returning them after so long, but the woman smiles and asks me if I'd like my refund in cash or on my bank card. The cash option is just too tempting, so I fish my card out of my wallet.

Most people would have gone home after that. Not me. My masochistic side thinks this would be a good time to challenge myself by mooching around the store for half an hour.

I'm not going to say it was easy, but at least I made it back to the car with nothing more than a sense of pride in myself.

Friday 11 August – Day 89

The great thing about doing PR for bands is that you get free tickets and tonight I'm taking advantage of that privilege.

Kevin has gone off on yet another boys' weekend. Golf this time, joined by Kirsty's husband, Davie. So, while the cats are away, the mice get to dress up and go into town.

Kirsty has promised to behave this evening. Last time I took her to see this band, she'd had a couple too many and I found her pogoing at the front of the stage, much to the amusement of the band, who were doing a slow number at the time.

When I tell the singer that we're going and that she'll just sway gently along to their tunes this time, he replies: 'I doubt that very much!'

But she remains true to her promise and the band's set is fantastic. It turns out to be the cheapest and most entertaining evening I've had for a while, proving that there's no reason that you can't enjoy yourself, even if you are on a no-frills budget.

Saturday 12 August – Day 90

Can my budget have one frill?

My wages are safely secreted in my bank account and even with my holiday spending being taken into account, I've managed to cut back enough to have a little extra cash.

Rules dictate that it has to go towards one of my credit cards, but my poor skin is crying out for a return to its usual brand. Why couldn't my upper dermis just be satisfied with a sugar scrub and a bit of olive oil?

I scooter into town, park (with the smug air of one who is exempt from parking fees) and skip to the department store to breathe in the chemical air of the beauty section, all perfumes and potions and the promise of perfection.

I'm intoxicated by it all as I stride to the Chanel counter, select the object of my desire and hand over my cash. With that simple action, the shopping drug has kicked in. As I dangle my purchase in its signature black-and-white bag my confidence starts to rocket, sending me into mooch overdrive for freebies.

Success in getting a generous sample of the new Chanel mascara, (the one I so wanted) sends me tripping over to the other counters where I don't get away quite so lightly.

I'm plonked on a stool and treated to a mini-makeover that leaves me resembling one of the dancers in the Kanye West 'Gold Digger' video. I depart with a sample of a face scrub (going to need that to get this slap off) and some highlighter. I wipe my gleaming face on my sleeve and marvel at how my lack of shame seems to grow with my lack of cash.

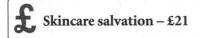

£ Skincare salvation – £21

Sunday 13 August – Day 91

Kevin came back from his golf trip this afternoon and even as I stood on tiptoe, puckering up with a 'welcome home' kiss, I couldn't help but spy the bags he was carrying.

He places the Ralph Lauren and Fatface bags on the kitchen work surface and I have to concentrate on the golf anecdotes, all the time pretending that I haven't spotted the tantalising totes.

I register odd words like 'birdie' and 'two putt', but all I can focus on are those bags.

Then he starts to show me the things he's bought for himself, pulling article after article out of the bags until I start thinking that there can't possibly be anything in them for me.

Just when I think I can't bear it any longer, I hear the magic words ... 'and these are for you'! He produces a glorious striped shirt from Ralph Lauren that fits perfectly (I have it on before he can even remove the pins from the collar), then follows it up with a dandy little Fatface T-shirt that clings in all the right places.

I have new clothes and I haven't even broken the rules!

Monday 14 August – Day 92

My friend, Alison, and I are bored with our old haunts and have been seeking out an establishment that is befitting of our (imagined) status.

As we only ever buy a tea and a hot chocolate, then huddle over them like a pair of old witches around a cauldron, I'm not quite sure what we perceive our status to be.

Our sights have settled on the nearby Malmaison – tranquil, classy and within our budget. I pull up a plush chair, upholstered in lush, soft leather and lower my plush bum, upholstered in Jaeger onto it. I'm making full use of one of my Mulberry bags, by placing it at the side of the table where everyone can see it. Unfortunately, this also means everyone can fall over it and it quickly gets tucked under the table, before I get sued for causing someone to break their ankle.

It's amazing how the right setting can make your usual beverage seem so much tastier. We posture like princesses (do princesses slurp?), marvel at the surprisingly small bill and synchronise our diaries for next time.

Tuesday 15 August – Day 93

I hurt my foot a couple of weeks ago and although it's agony to wear my towering heels, I tell myself that childbearing must be worse and force myself to endure the pain.

Most days, I wear my trainers when I go for lunch, but today the suit trousers I'm wearing are too long for flats and I have to teeter along the road, biting my lip and humming to pretend that my throbbing foot is merely the work of a vivid imagination.

I'm doing quite well until I remember that my bank card and spare cash are in my jacket pocket and that my jacket is lying on the back of the chair in my office. The prospect of having to go back for it is too much and just as I'm about to enter into a wail of theatrical proportions, it occurs to me that I'm a serial change chucker. Notes get folded neatly back in my wallet, but coins get launched straight into my bag, rattling around and finding gaps in the lining to hide in.

Dragging my useless limb behind me, I rush to a quiet corner of the M&S food hall and start tipping the contents of my bag on to the floor, sifting through the piles of receipts and rubbish, until I've gathered up enough cash for a sandwich.

Okay, so a foot bandage might have been a better purchase, but my lunch tasted all the better for the trauma and my bag got a much needed clear-out.

Wednesday 16 August – Day 94

We have no hot water.

The boiler has coughed and spluttered to a halt and suddenly we're living in the Dark Ages.

I've never had to endure a truly cold shower before and so fool myself into thinking that it can't be that bad.

After three minutes of crying and making some rather disturbing involuntary shrieks each time the cold water hits me, I change my mind about how bad it is and call the plumber.

He obviously senses the hysteria in my voice and promises to come out as soon as possible.

Thursday 17 August – Day 95

Promises, promises …

Still no sign of the plumber. I really can't face another cold shower and Kevin is deeply concerned that the neighbours may think I'm being tortured if I start making those noises again, so I start boiling up pots on the stove to fill the bath.

Funny how the bath seems a lot bigger when you're trying to fill it with a saucepan. An hour and a half later, I've worn a path from the cooker to the loo and only managed to produce about four inches of lukewarm water to dabble in.

Suffice to say that after yesterday, it feels like the epitome of luxury and I even have the nerve to throw in a splash of bubble bath.

Friday 18 August – Day 96

At last the plumber arrives.

He tinkers about, sighs a little and tells me it'll be Monday before he can get the right part.

It's all too much for me and after throwing a tantrum that would put most three-year-olds to shame, I convince (force) him to go and source the part.

Two hours later, I'm standing under a hot shower.

I'm so happy that I throw caution to the wind and celebrate by opening a fresh bar of Nivea soap.

Such simple pleasures!

Saturday 19 August – Day 97

There are parts of me that embrace city living and others that are just screaming out to escape to a country cottage by a river. The latter has been most obvious lately.

I always do this during the summer months. Dreaming of a garden with ducks dabbling around, laying eggs for our breakfast, while I pick the ripened tomatoes from the plants I grew from seed, Kevin harvests the honey from our busy (non-stinging) bees, and Hobbs lies dozing away the day on a Cath Kidston-covered beanbag.

But no matter how unrealistic those dreams may be, the reality is that we can't move anywhere with the burden of my debt hanging over us, so Kevin sets me a challenge. If I clear as much of my debt as possible over the next eighteen months, we can move.

There's no hiding from the fact that my debt affects us both. Money may not buy you happiness, but it certainly gives you better options.

Monday 21 August – Day 99

I've promised a colleague that I'll take her to a wholesale warehouse I have a card for, but what seemed like a good idea at the time has suddenly become a test of strength.

Having deliberately avoided the damn place with its ludicrously low-priced goods and tempting offers for things that I really don't need, (but have to buy anyway because they're such a bargain) I'm now gaily marching through the door, pushing a trolley that's just begging to be filled.

Stationery gets me every time, but after wheeling a pack of coloured pens (what exactly do you do with a yellow biro?), along with a box of notepads up and down a couple of aisles, I suddenly come to my senses and put them back.

When I do finally get to the till, I have only a few essential food items to pay for.

It's not necessarily a shopping trip I want to repeat every week, but every little test that I set myself (and pass) makes me increasingly confident that I can see this year out.

Tuesday 22 August – Day 100

Hobbs got bitten by a much larger dog today.

It just charged across the road and bit him hard on his side before I could stop it. It's a dog I'd never seen before and never want to see again.

Hobbs wasn't badly hurt, but the sight of him cowering and shaking left me in tears and feeling helpless that I hadn't been able to protect him.

Luckily, we were on our way to the pet shop, so when we arrived, the owner and I checked him over and put ointment on the area where his fur had been pulled out and his skin grazed. He was still shaken and flinched when we touched the area, causing me to well up again.

I broke my rule and bought a toy to cheer him up, then walked home with tears still pricking my eyes, while he trotted along at my side, doing his level best to be brave.

Wednesday 23 August – Day 101

I'm not feeling very safe after yesterday's incident and having been badly bitten by a dog myself a few years ago, I vow that it's not going to happen again.

I get on the internet and within in a couple of minutes find what I'm looking for – a doggy version of pepper spray.

While £9.99 seems a small price to pay for peace of mind, does it make me a vigilante? Will I be trying to buy a gun next, declaring my right to bear arms? I remember that in

Britain we only have the right to bare arms, and even then, only if they're toned and tanned and the temperature's above freezing.

I want to protect Hobbs and myself from attack, but feel I can't buy the spray. I log off and try to think of an alternative.

Then I remember that there is something that dogs hate, something that sends Hobbs loopy any time it gets used around him. Hairspray!

A quick rummage through the bathroom cabinet and I find my dog deterrent. It's even a handbag size that fits perfectly in my pocket, so if it's a particularly windy day I can preen as I protect.

Thursday 24 August – Day 102

While I'm wandering around during my lunch hour today I notice that one of the shops is doing a big 'buy one, get one free' promotion.

This makes me wonder …

If I were to take them up on their kind offer, then return one item for a refund, would I get all my money back and still have wangled keeping the free one?

These are the bizarre things that are now running through my head, filling the gap where Gap used to be.

Friday 25 August – Day 103

For the past few weeks I've been limiting myself to £5 pocket money a day and it really seems to be working.

I'm managing to pay for my lunch and transport without going over my limit, and on some days I've even been under budget. This could be another way to help pay for a few of the goods I can't go without.

If I can put aside enough of my pocket money each day, then I can totally justify sticking with my posh skincare.

I know I keep going back to this, but it's been a real issue for me since I started this experiment and part of me feels I should have just opted for a budget range and lived with the spotty consequences.

But instead of feeling constant nagging guilt over using Chanel, maybe I can set myself a new challenge to save more daily and solve my dermatalogical dilemma.

Sunday 27 August – Day 105

Working weekends really does save you money, but it doesn't stop me having to drag myself away from town each day when it's packed with people going about the serious sport of browsing and buying.

Today was no exception, but I was a woman on a mission. And that mission meant having to leave town straight after my shift.

An old dance hall on my route home is being pulled down and I wanted to stop off to see if I could scrounge a souvenir. So, I scoot across town in the hope of catching the workmen before they shut up site for the day.

I had my heart set on an 'A' from the sign that had blazed above the main entrance for over half a century, but when I get there everything has been reduced to rubble.

All I can identify is a child's shoe that looked as though it had been there since the forties and it seems a sorry end for such a beautiful old building.

It also makes me think that no matter how grand we may seem on the outside with our fabulous clothes, cars and jewels, we all end up like that old building eventually.

Reduced to rubble, with just a few memories to show for all those years.

Monday 28 August – Day 106

I forgot to take my lip balm to work today and although it can't be classed as an international incident, it still causes me to fret.

The minute I realise my bag is bereft of balm I start chewing at my lips. It takes me five minutes to have them raw and bleeding.

Can I justify going out at lunchtime and buying a cheapy Chapstick? Not really.

In a last desperate measure, I ferret about in my desk drawers and there, lurking at the back is an old Bloom gloss.

I dread to think how long it's been there, but it's saved the day and a couple of quid.

I slather it on, ignoring the random bits of fluff welded to the container and savour the moment, smacking my lips together like a demented goldfish.

Tuesday 29 August – Day 107

It's my fairy goddaughter's first birthday today.

As she's on the other side of the country and I won't get to see her, I decide to call and screech down the phone. It was meant to be a rendition of 'Happy Birthday' and I'm just hopeful that their little ears aren't quite fully developed at twelve months.

Although shopping is off the cards for me, I don't see why I have to deprive other people and as the whole point of this year is for me to live as normal a life as possible, the purchase of a Moulin Roty pull-along elephant isn't exactly breaking the rules.

Sometimes buying for someone else is actually more satisfying and just the thought of her teetering along on cheeky, chubby little legs with her new toy is enough to make me smile.

> **£** Present for podgy kneed little tot – £35

Wednesday 30 August – Day 108

A day off work in the week means that I'm left to my own devices and that's when the desire to shop kicks in. If I go out, I'm tempted by the shops. If I stay in, I'm tempted by internet shopping.

To distract me from both, I decide to walk Hobbs and get a newspaper, but while we're out, it occurs to me that I should stop seeing the internet as the enemy and start to embrace it as a friend who can save me money.

Why am I buying the paper, when I can log on to an almost endless number of publications?

Admittedly, it isn't quite the same as brewing a good strong pot of coffee and settling down at the table with a crisp newspaper, but for now it's another little way of saving money and if we're paying for the internet connection then we may as well get our money's worth.

5

Entrusted with the bank card ...

September 2006

Debt to date = £29,968.33

Saturday 2 September – Day 111

Months ago, Kevin bought a couple of Robbie Williams concert tickets with the intention of selling them on the internet and making a tidy little profit.

What he hadn't bargained on was the tickets arriving just a week before the gig – making it too late to sell them – and that they would include hospitality. To top it all, Basement Jaxx were listed as the support act. How could we not go?!

But how could we justify £110 for two tickets?

The rules of the shopping ban dictates that I can't pay half, so we compromised and I agreed for my ticket to be part of my birthday present. A fair deal, I reckon, and it turned out to be a night not to be missed.

Basement Jaxx were sensational, the stage set was breathtaking, the atmosphere was incredible and there, over a sea of pink cowboy hats, was Robbie strutting on the stage like a funky Norman Wisdom.

But the highlight of the evening came from a rather unexpected source.

Cameras were scanning the crowd and on finding herself featuring largely on the screens, a woman decided to lift her top, flash her enormous breasts and for a little extra effect give them a long and lingering lick.

I never thought I'd see an entertainer of Robbie's magnitude rendered speechless, but along with the 15,000 strong audience, he was.

Sunday 3 September – Day 112

We have a new neighbour – a really quiet guy – who decided to turn up the volume a little last night and have a house-warming party.

It was nothing that earplugs couldn't drown out and our ears were ringing anyway from the noise of the concert. Besides, he'd invited all of the tenants and if your neighbours can't have the odd party at the weekend without you moaning, then you really should live in a detached house.

But the sight that met me this morning made me think very differently.

It's bad enough having to work on a Sunday, but when you go to fetch your scooter from the back door and find that a party guest has thrown up over the bannister and all over your little two-wheeler, it just gets a lot worse.

I can't justify taking it to the hand-wash garage and paying someone to clean it, and anyway, I'd still have to ride it there (covered in puke). So, armed with disinfectant, a bucket of water and a very long-handled brush, I set to work, then ride into the office with my bottom hovering an inch above the seat and wearing a face like a cat's arse!

Monday 4 September – Day 113

My magazine has arrived through the mail again today, even though I was convinced the subscription had finished.

Perhaps they've forgotten after all, and I'll just keep finding it there on the doormat every month.

The honest part of me thinks I should phone them to say, but I'm overcome by greed and my good fortune, so lie on the couch instead devouring every page with guilty pleasure.

Tuesday 5 September – Day 114

I'm still reeling from the scooter-sick incident and wrinkling my nose every time I have to park my derrière on the area where the offending substance was, so you can imagine how delighted I was to leave work today and find a huge bird poo on the seat.

If one more person tells me that's lucky, I swear I'll strike them!

It's not bloody lucky when you're wearing your good suit, let me tell you.

Wednesday 6 September – Day 115

Okay, okay, maybe it has brought me luck.

Today I had to come to terms with the fact that the end was nigh for my dog-walking trainers. When the air-cushioned bit at the back wears away and pebbles sneak into the gap, then you know it's time to consign them to the bin.

I tried using the excuse that the rattling was handy for Hobbs as he could hear where I was in the dark, but then Kevin pointed out that being a dog, Hobbs can see in the dark and my whole argument fell apart.

The lucky part comes courtesy of my previous desire to buy two of everything that I thought was a bargain (and occasionally even when I thought it was a rip-off, but couldn't decide on just one colour). Hence the fact that there are a pair of pristine, snowy white, virginal versions of the binned pair snuggled up in a shoebox at the bottom of my wardrobe.

It's almost as good as having just bought them and I spring along the pavement dazzling the dog and his night vision with their gleaming whiteness.

Thursday 7 September – Day 116

Having harped on incessantly for the past few days about houses that I've seen up for sale, I thought I should check out our mortgage situation to see how much we can stretch to. How I wish I hadn't!

There's nothing like a chat with the bank to bring you back to your senses.

It turns out that my debt means we'd qualify for even less of a mortgage than we currently have.

This is the biggest reality check yet and however flippantly I may have started this challenge, I now realise just how seriously I have to take it if I want to have any kind of stability in the future.

Friday 8 September – Day 117

I always think that part of the joy of opening a shop must be coming up with the name and if that's the case, then the owner of the 'Wizard of Paws' pet shop must have been like a dog with two tails.

I've been entrusted with the bank card for our joint account, on the condition that I go to the pet shop, get Hobbs' birthday present and come home without stopping along the way to buy shoes or (as I'm passing the garage) that little, black Mini with the silver stripe over the bonnet.

As it turns out I could easily clear the account in just this one shop, but I control myself and leave with a Bubble Buddy, a stuffed dinosaur that snores when you shake it, home-baked dog biscuits (chicken flavour), a squeaky piglet, a set of chewy keys and a frisbee.

Had I been out of control, I'd have added the jacket with hood trimmed in faux fur, bandana, collar studded with silver terriers, and the lead to match. Hobbs would've worn none of these and Kevin would've made me return them all, so at least I saved myself that embarrassment.

Having viewed the bulging bags and rehidden the bank card, Kevin – rather unkindly – points out that the dog can only play with one toy at a time and perhaps the frisbee would have sufficed.

Seems my idea of control and his are very different things.

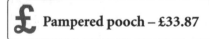 **Pampered pooch – £33.87**

Sunday 10 September – Day 119

For some reason, I only ever read my horoscope at the weekend. Perhaps I imagine it'll give me the foresight I need to see me through the week ahead, but like most people, I only ever believe it if it tells me something good.

Today's predication was so bang on, it was like being shot between the eyes. It was about how you should live each day at a time and really savour that moment without rushing ahead to the next thing.

BSB, that would have been one of the horoscopes I would have rubbished, but today it made sense to me.

I've been so preoccupied with what I can have next – what coat I should be buying for the season ahead, what heel height is ideal for winter when I'm still in my summer flip-flops – that I haven't been able to enjoy what I already had.

Have I just treated my whole life like that? Desperate to grab the next big thing without taking into account all the little things already there, waiting to be savoured.

It makes me wonder how long I've been blinkered, and how many incredible moments I've missed as I've tossed everything aside in a bid to get the latest bag.

Monday 11 September – Day 120

It's the fifth anniversary of the Twin Towers atrocity. I'm not sure 'anniversary' is really the appropriate word for such a tragedy – you usually associate it with far happier occasions.

I worked in a newsroom when it happened and can remember with horrible clarity how the situation unfolded. The stunned silence as we watched the second plane strike.

Today in a different office, with different colleagues, we fall silent again as we watch the memorial service and I think about how lucky I really am.

Tuesday 12 September – Day 121

As I scooter into work this morning, I pass the shops getting ready to open and think of the days that followed the attacks on America and the words of the then mayor of New York, Rudolph Giuliani.

What did he urge the New Yorkers to do? To get back out there, to live their lives as normally as possible and to stop being afraid.

And presumably that also meant getting back to shopping. Almost all American retail chains closed on September 11th and every single one of them was open again by the next day.

Wednesday 13 September – Day 122

I have two new pieces of reading material today.

One of them is a *Harper's Bazaar*, donated by Alison, which is lovingly thumbed and has pages turned down so I'm sure not to miss the things that she thinks I'll get excited about. The other is a book purchased by my beloved.

The *Harper's Bazaar* I'm clearly thrilled about, as a) I'm not allowed to buy magazines, and b) because although tempted by the delightful dresses, even I'm not deluded enough to think I can afford them and therefore it doesn't cause me too much pain.

The book is by Alvin Hall and is all about managing money. It's a gift from Kevin and is so indicative of his support and attempts to understand me.

I kiss him thank you and promise to read it in a bid to improve my financial standing and our future together, then skip off to run a bath, so I can disappear beneath the bubbles and lose myself in literature.

(Obviously I take the *Harper's* with me; I couldn't possibly let Alvin see me in the bath.)

Thursday 14 September – Day 123
Alison admits to me that for days she's been trying to pluck up the courage to ask me to order her a shirt from Charles Tyrwhitt.

I'd left the brochure on her desk a couple of weeks ago after I couldn't bear to look at it any longer without actually licking the cover out of sheer lust for its glorious contents.

She could order it herself, but I have an account and therefore am eligible for a discount. It's a well-known fact that clothing sits so much better when you know you got a little money off, so we congregate over the catalogue and select which slinky number she desires the most.

For all her fears that she's going to set me off on a shopping splurge of my own, she's wrong and I'm more than happy to do the dirty deed on her behalf.

This way I get the thrill but not the bill.

Friday 15 September – Day 125
I'm off to visit my friend, Gordon, in his swanky new office and as I've been promised a specially selected coffee, I offer to supply the cakes.

One of his colleagues is something of a coffee connoisseur and magics up a different blend each day to suit the mood of the office, so the pressure's on for me to get the perfect pastries.

My old style was to dash into M&S and grab the nearest box of biscuits, but now as I'm savouring any excuse to shop, I dither about in the local bakery selecting a different cake for each person.

Delighted with both myself and my selection, I jump on the scooter and set off.

It's only when I arrive that things start to go wrong. With the cake box in one hand, I try to pull my helmet off with the other and catch the end of my nose on the hard plastic lip. Agony! I've taken a chunk of skin off the end of my nose and my eyes are streaming.

I compose myself, enter the office and hand over the cake box, which I now see I've been carrying upside down.

As we sit, sipping today's superb caffeine blend, picking bits of icing and cream off the cardboard cake box lid, I feel I should say something about my DIY rhinoplasty before he does.

'Sorry about the state of my nose.'

'Don't be silly', he says, pretending he hadn't noticed. 'What is it anyway? A spot?'

I realise I can either lick my wounds or the lid of the box and opt for the latter.

Saturday 16 September – Day 126

Another working weekend and Kevin has come up trumps.

(Am I starting to value him more, now that I'm focusing on something other than fashion?)

After a hugely frustrating day, I scooter home in the pouring rain to be met by a perfectly prepared cocktail, a cigar and the smell of dinner wafting from the kitchen.

He hugs me, hangs up my jacket and I smile with the satisfaction of having finally figured out what 'priceless' really means.

Sunday 17 September – Day 127

I still have to get the wrapping paper and card for Hobbs' birthday, so leave for work a little earlier than usual and drop into the shops on the way.

I'm strolling along the road with my purchases when I see the actor Joe McGann, chatting in the street on his mobile. People are passing him, nudging each other and pointing at 'that man from the telly'.

I'm desperate to ask for his autograph but can't interrupt his call and have to walk away.

Years ago, when I worked in the newsroom of a radio station, I kept an autograph book for the dog, which visiting celebs would be asked to sign. It drew some rather strange looks and comments, but no one ever refused and as a result, Hobbs has quite a cool collection of autographs and signed pictures.

It almost went horribly wrong one day when he was still a puppy and had been feeling poorly. The vet recommended we keep an eye on him and my boss kindly allowed me to bring him in to work, where we built a natty little pen from upturned desks. Filled with blankets and toys, it was an ideal canine crèche.

I'd popped to the loo for two seconds and came back to find Hobbs being carried around and licking the face of a guy in a hat. As I walked over to warn him that he was ingesting poorly puppy germs, he turned round and I found myself staring at Mark Owen.

I spent weeks scanning the papers to make sure that no dreadful disease had befallen him (Mark, not Hobbs) as he launched his solo singing career: especially when it turned out that the dog had been suffering from a throat infection.

Monday 18 September – Day 128

Hobbs' fourth birthday!

As a treat we're taking him to the Lake District. It's really a treat for the three of us, as Kevin and I both have a few days holiday left to take and figure it's the perfect excuse for a trip away while the weather's still quite good. Also, it's not entirely practical to send the dog off to a hotel on his own.

First though, we have to go through the present-opening ceremony. Paper is strewn over the kitchen floor and I skip around like a demented fairy trying to entice my fur kid to play with his bacon-flavoured bubbles.

Nothing.

Having spent more money on the Bubble Buddy than anything else, I'm determined to prove to Kevin and Hobbs that it was worth every penny.

Perhaps I'm not selling it enough, perhaps if I make small whoops of excitement as I skip. Still nothing.

I finally get the message when Hobbs throws me a disdainful look and rips one of the horns from his stuffed snoring triceratops.

Time to pack the car …

Tuesday 19 September – Day 129

It's a perfect day pottering around the Lakes. The colours are just starting to turn as we head into autumn and with the tourist season pretty much over, we feel like we have the place to ourselves.

When I was little, I had a pedal car modelled on Donald Campbell's Bluebird. I think my dad must have been a big fan and somehow his admiration of the great man seems to have passed on to me, so we pay a visit to Coniston Water, where the Bluebird lay on the bottom for so many years – a tomb to the driver who sank beneath the surface with her.

It's a lot eerier and sadder than I had expected. There's a little cafe by the edge of the water and just a few feet away is a stone that marks Donald Campbell's passing. I feel so sad as I stand reading it, listen to the voices of the people around me who've just arrived on a coach trip and until seeing the stone appear to have had no idea of the significance of the area they were visiting.

There are little Bluebird souvenirs in the cafe and although I'm desperate to buy one to replace my now long-gone child-hood toy, I know I can't part with the cash.

Instead I take some photographs of Hobbs paddling around in the lake and Kevin lifts the sombre mood by commenting that the dog appears to be swimming faster than usual.

Wednesday 20 September – Day 130

We drive the whole way up to Glasgow with fingers and toes crossed after the car springs a leak just a few miles into our journey back.

With industrial strength radiator fixer, a lot of nail biting and water top-up stops every half-hour, we finally make it home.

One of our stops just happened to coincide with the junction that takes you to the outlet village at Gretna. BSB, I'd have been out of the car like a greyhound from its trap and racing towards Ralph Lauren and LK Bennett, throwing women and children aside as I went. Today though I just couldn't be bothered and even felt relieved to get back to the car without buying anything. At least it saved me the torment of being told to 'take it back'.

Back home, we unpack the steaming wreck that was our car, then flop onto the couch and flick on the news to see that the presenter, Richard Hammond, has been seriously injured trying to break the land speed record. It sends shivers up our spines to see that so soon after visiting the site where Britain's former land and water speed record holder lost his life.

Friday 22 September – Day 132
Alison's shirt has arrived. I'm tempted to open the box and pretend I'd thought it was something else.

Dammit, I can't! Opening the box would lead to me taking it out of the cellophane, which would lead to me holding it up in the mirror (to see the colour against my skin tone), to trying it on, to wearing it out somewhere ...

Now I know how Pandora must have felt.

Instead I entrust the box to Kevin and head into the office to work the public holiday in a bid to boost my wages and pay off a little extra debt this month.

Saturday 23 September – Day 133

Getting my hair cut today, I opt for a slightly shorter style, hoping it'll take longer to grow in before my next trim, but knowing it'll probably just go out of style quicker.

My attitude to having my haircut has changed recently. Because I can no longer book on a whim and pay with my credit card, I have to make my appointment according to whether I have the money in my bank account or not.

Subsequently, if I don't have my tresses tended, I don't feel groomed and my whole self-image sets off on a downward spiral, making me want to rush out and buy all of the things that I imagine will make me feel and look better.

This vicious circle has made it vital that I keep my spending in check to leave me with enough cash to cover the cost of my coiffure.

Suddenly something as simple as a haircut has started to feel like an achievement.

£ Financing fine follicles – £32

Monday 25 September – Day 134

One of my credit cards is internet-based, which means I don't receive a paper statement from them.

Having mastered the art of reading the statements from my other cards in recent months, I feel I can now cope with logging on to check this one.

This is a card that hasn't been used for around a year, after I ran the account up to its limit and then promptly lost the little piece of plastic somewhere among the clutter in the flat, so I wasn't exactly overjoyed to see that I'd paid off a grand total of just £41.

Had I been contributing only a fiver a month, I'd have understood, but there's £60 a month going towards that account! It seems that for several months the interest they added had been putting me over the credit limit, giving them every opportunity to start wading in with the charges and pushing my balance ever upwards.

I frantically call round my three other cards, transferring as much as I can to each of them. Thankfully none of them have been used since May and have been cleared enough to accommodate the remainder from my rogue card.

Laziness in not checking my statement has cost me dearly and I have no one to blame but myself.

Tuesday 26 September – Day 135

Alison's in today, so I wedge the Tyrwhitt shirt box into the carrier on my scooter to take her order to the office. I feel like a sort of posh pizza delivery service.

She tries to smile as I hand over the box that now looks like an origami attempt by Mike Tyson in mittens.

As she takes it from me, I'm momentarily dazzled by the rock that's adorning her finger. It's the kind of sparkler that can blind you at 50 paces and is a gift for her tenth wedding anniversary. I don't want to say anything crass about cost, but it must have been a small fortune. To be fair to her, if her husband had got it from a cracker, she'd still have loved it and him.

I can't wait to get home and enthuse about it to Kevin. I even try drawing it. After half an hour, his eyes are starting to roll and flicker.

'He must have spent thousands on that', I say, as he tries to escape to the loo, knowing what's coming next.

'I'll never get anything like that, will I?' I'm pushing my luck now, following him along the hall as his pace quickens.

He makes it to the sanctuary of the loo and closes the door on me, from behind which I hear: 'Not if cost thousands, you bloody won't.'

Wednesday 27 September – Day 136

Instead of trawling the town today, oohing and aahing at all the things we can't buy, Verity and I decide to go for the long leisurely lunch approach.

This makes a lot more sense when you take into account the fact that she's eight months pregnant and sitting is definitely a good option right now, and that I'm a retail wreck and shopping is definitely not a good option right now.

I'm desperate to hear the latest update on her rock-star neighbour and she doesn't disappoint.

Today's tale involves her hormone-induced mood swings and his apparent inability to move his bin bags.

It all started off innocently enough with Verity popping across the landing to politely enquire when the offending items were being removed.

And perhaps if he'd answered the door the first time she knocked on it, things could have been very different. As it was, he came to the door on her third attempt, all bed-head hair and half-closed eyes to be met by a screaming harpy, hell bent on a clutter-free close.

Verity: 'When are these going to be taken away?'

Rock God (still half asleep): 'Ummm, when's the uplift?'

Verity: 'Tuesday morning.'

Rock God (still on Australian time): 'Right, so what day is it today?'

Verity: 'TUESDAY!! AFTERNOON!'

With that, she turned on her heel and stomped back across the landing and into her flat, leaving him confused and probably a little terrified.

'I thought he stayed at his big posh pad in the country?' I say, trying to make light of the situation.

She looks guiltily up from her latte. 'Well, I think he does now.'

Thursday 28 September – Day 137

I've got my six-month check-up at the dentist and I'm dreading it!

I do this every time. Stuffing my face with sweets and chocolate between check-ups then spending the week before my appointment overcompensating by flossing my gums into a bloody mess and scrubbing so hard that my toothbrush bristles splay.

I'm sitting in the chair trying to form words around my dentist's fingers – without either biting her or drooling on myself – while she asks me what I've been up to. I'm also mentally trying to tally the cost of the visit, knowing that any extra work is all my own doing.

Eventually the agony is over and the bill presented. I try squinting to see if that makes it look any less frightening and then see it's the check-up only, with no further work needed.

I resist the urge to kiss the dentist with my minty fresh breath and instead – beaming broadly – reward myself with a swish new head for my electric toothbrush.

£ Toothy treats – £31.40

Friday 29 September – Day 138
This morning I open the door to:

Jo Malone, Johnnie Boden, Charles Tyrwhitt, Bombay Duck, Mulberry, Toast and The White Company.

All crammed onto the doormat, all begging me to embrace them and run away on a shopping spree.

When did they decide to get together and gang up on me en masse?!

I toy with them momentarily, impressed by their efforts to seduce me, before sweeping them into my arms, carrying them lovingly over the threshold … and dumping them in the recycle bin.

Saturday 30 September – Day 139
In a bid to give myself even more of an incentive to save, we go to look at a new house that's up for sale in the leafy suburbs near our little flat.

It's in a quiet street and although far from being our ideal home, it's what we could afford if I cleared my debt. We go from room to room, trying to imagine the decor and all the little ways we'd put our personal touch into the empty boxes with their cold, bare walls.

Kevin's quieter than usual when we get home and I watch him over the top of the newspaper I'm pretending to read.

'What's wrong?' I ask, dreading that the answer relates to my spending and how it's holding us back. He shrugs. 'Is it something I've done?' I venture. He shakes his head.

Then it all comes out …

Seeing the house today made Kevin realise that even he has des-res desires above his station. His dream of us in a sand-stone villa – with a slate-floored kitchen and an Aga; Hobbs sleeping peacefully at our feet; while classical music floats in the air, intermingling with the smell of a Sunday roast – has been dashed.

He's been hit by a double whammy. It's a bad day when you discover not only that you can't afford the house of your dreams, but you can barely afford the one of your nightmares.

6

I deserve a little treat ...

October 2006

Debt to date = £29,132.84

Sunday 1 October – Day 140

I think my stress levels may be lowering.

My ability to go from calm to stratospheric hysterical in point three of a second seems to be waning and with it I'm starting to notice a change in my attitude. My high-school teachers would be so relieved, if a little bemused that it's taken so long.

My desperation to own everything that I see is fading and so it seems, is my anxiety. And as my anxiety levels drop, so does my aggressive streak, that used to leave me lashing out like a cornered rat whenever Kevin even attempted to ask me how I was able to afford all of the things I was filling our flat with.

Money, or the lack of it, is no longer the first thing on my mind when I wake up in the morning.

Even waking to the sound of the alarm after a blissful sleep is fairly novel for me. BSB it wasn't unusual for me to lie awake all night in a sweat, panicking about how I was going to pay the bills and still be able to keep up with the Joneses, get 'the bag' for the season and, most of all, keep the awful truth from Kevin.

I feel I'm more in control now, more honest with Kevin, and in doing that, I'm finally being honest with myself.

Monday 2 October – Day 141

For some time now I've been a bit worried that my grooming standards may be slipping and an incident this morning really brought matters to a (black)head.

When you own a mud magnet of a dog, you don't tend to walk them wearing couture, but perhaps I've taken the relaxed look a bit too far.

After a morning walk in the park, a romp through the mud and a good old snuffle that allowed Hobbs to collect his pmail*, we start back down the road.

Halfway down, the street is closed to cars and a group of workmen are toiling in the autumn sun. As I approach, they stop what they're doing, lean on their shovels and turn to look at me. I smile (okay, I'll admit I was pouting a little) and walk past, to hear the immortal line ...

'Look at that lovely wee dog.'

Initially I'm puffed up with pride that I have such a delightful-looking dog, but then it hits me. Workmen used to whistle at me! I've been upstaged by a canine that, at best, resembles a burst cushion!

I then worry the whole way home in case it was actually me they were referring to.

*We have email, dogs have p(ee)mail. That's why you find them snuffling round lampposts, up trees and in hedges – all the places they pick up and leave their messages ... you get the idea.

Tuesday 3 October – Day 142

I'm sitting in waiting for the delivery of the lovely grub I've ordered online.

I know it might seem lazy, but (and I'm going to get all serious here) there are really good reasons to buy your food that way.

Firstly, it's delivered to you, saving your petrol and helping the environment, because they have one van on the road instead of many cars heading to and from the supermarket.

Then there's the benefit of knowing exactly how much you've spent: I know for a fact that I'm not the only person who has gone out for olives and come back £45 down and without the very thing I went to buy in the first place.

But best of all, it cuts out temptation. I can look for the things I want to buy without passing aisles of stuff that I don't. And I can select the supermarket's own brand without feeling that someone will be sizing up my trolley, tut-tutting over its lack of labels.

My purchases are free of peer pressure *and* I'm saving myself a sizeable sum.

Wednesday 4 October – Day 143

I get a call this morning from an old friend offering me a job.

It's a few thousand pounds more a year and he says he'll leave me to think about his offer. He's barely finished his sentence when I've bought the sandstone villa that Kevin so desires and am clacking my way across the slate floor in my Christian Louboutin shoes, their red soles flashing against the polished black of the stone. I pick up the keys to my convertible, fling my Furla bag into the footwell, where it nestles in the plush carpet, and drive to the office.

What the hell am I thinking about?!

He's offering me my old job back, the one I left to take up my current post. This is the post I so desperately wanted that I stressed myself into chest pains and spent the journey to the interview thinking: 'I'm having a heart attack, but at least I'm having it in my best suit.'

For all of my boasts that I've got my spending under control and started sorting myself out, I'm still able to create a Martha Stewart lifestyle with a few thousand pounds extra and an overactive imagination.

Thursday 5 October – Day 145

I'm working late tonight and end up chatting to a journalist who's called for some more background on a press release I've put out.

He asks how we all enjoyed the Lakes and if the dog had a good birthday. I tell him about the trip and how Hobbs sulked after finding out that he could have stayed at Malmaison, had his own comfy basket and logoed dishes – all for £10 extra – and how we'll probably take him there next year.

'Malmaison!!' he spits. 'Jesus Christ, if you're prepared to spend that kind of money, I'll sit in a basket in the corner, licking my balls!'

(Must keep him on my speed dial in case I ever throw a party that requires a contortionist.)

Friday 6 October – Day 146

The noise of a single firework within a five-mile radius is enough to send Hobbs running for cover.

Last year, Kevin and I did everything we could to calm him, as they exploded into the sky above our flat in the weeks before and after Bonfire Night.

All of our efforts were in vain, so this year we're planning early. So far, we've purchased a *Music for Pets* CD that's meant to lull and soothe (all crashy and screechy instruments have been removed to enhance the listening pleasure of your four-legged friend) and I've transformed one of his comfy baskets by building a cage over the top and using an old duvet to form a kind of soundproof igloo.

Kevin and I have each been in the igloo several times, making enthusiastic noises about how cosy/quiet/tranquil it is, while Hobbs stands outside resolutely refusing to place even a paw inside.

Today the pièce de résistance in our fight against firework fear arrived. Instead of tranquillisers, the vet has suggested a device that emits pheromones to calm your canine. All you do is plug it in and ta-da – one peaceful pet.

I'd love to know if it works, but between the CD and the plug-in, neither Kevin nor I have been able to stay awake long enough to see the dog's reaction.

Saturday 7 October – Day 147

Thank heaven for wedding lists.

Stress-free shopping and a guarantee that the gift is something the happy couple actually want. I mean, how many times can you write a thank-you card for a bale of bath sheets when there are acres of towelling engulfing your home and threatening to take over the garden?

That's why I nearly have a fit today when I call my mother to find out what she's buying to celebrate my cousin, Melinda's forthcoming nuptials, and she responds with: 'Towels.'

'Are they on the list?' I ask, knowing that I've already logged on to the internet, bought my gift and failed to glimpse a single centimetre of fluffy absorbent fabric along the many and varied items.

After her explaining in pained tones that she doesn't have a computer (I know this) and me explaining that she can do the ordering by phone (she didn't know that), she hangs up.

Ten minutes later, she's back on the phone, high on purchasing power and shrieking that she's bought a Brabantia bin.

And they say you can't teach an old dog new tricks ...

Sunday 8 October – Day 148

There is half a hundredweight of fruit in our kitchen.

The kitchen work surfaces are groaning under the burden of bag after bag of rhubarb, damsons, plums and apples, while Kevin stands at the sink lovingly washing and rebagging them with the excited air of a squirrel packing its last few nuts into winter storage.

I've been noticing that as I become less consumer-crazed, Kevin's becoming more environmentally friendly. He cycles to work almost every day, recycles every object he can and has now raided a friend's orchard for its organic produce.

He starts reeling off all the things that he'll be making. Jam, apple sauce, apple crumble, rhubarb crumble, plum jelly and – just as I'm starting to think that I'm living with that Hugh Fearnley-Whatsit bloke, he announces the one thing that makes me prick up my ears – damson gin!

Go Greens!!

Monday 9 October – Day 148

I attempt to make a smoothie for breakfast using some of Kevin's fruit harvest.

It's a little on the bitter side – a bit like myself after discovering that every available inch of the freezer has been packed with plums, leaving no room for stockpiling the necessary winter store of Ben & Jerry's ice cream.

Tuesday 10 October – Day 149

No matter how little spending I do, or however much I think I may be weaning myself off uncontrollable shopping, I don't think I'll ever be able to stop equating everything to shoes and handbags.

You know – a week's grocery shopping is the equivalent of a quarter of a pair of Manolos or the dog's booster jag is a tenth of a Chloe Paddington.

Perhaps I'll always do it. There I'll be, tottering off to the post office working out the Prada-loafer percentage my pension entitles me to.

Wednesday 11 October – Day 150

One of my workmates has suggested that as I'm doing fairly well at controlling my credit-card compulsion, maybe I should reward myself with a little gift each pay day.

What a good idea! Not that it hasn't already crossed my mind, but someone else recommending it makes it so much better. After all, if it isn't all my idea, then I can absolve myself of most of the guilt before I've even hit the shops. Oh, this is looking good.

'Go on', I say, dusting down my wallet for action. 'What do you propose?'

'Well, a hundred pounds seems fair.'

'What?! I can't possibly spend that.'

'OK', she counters, '50 then.'

But suddenly even that seems like an awful lot.

At the start of this year, I'd have thought nothing of spending upwards of £50 during my lunch hour, but now it all comes down to payments towards my debt and £600 worth of 'well dones' a year can't be justified any more.

I stuff the moths back in my wallet and shelve the whole idea.

Thursday 12 October – Day 151

I'm still thinking about how much I deserve a little treat as I wander around the Clarins department today, when I see that they have an offer on the go.

All I have to do is buy two items and they give me three lovely freebies. Three! It's so generous of them, it'd be rude of me not to join in.

I pop a body wash and deodorant in my basket, then go to look for something for lunch while I'm there. As I swing the basket to and fro, the red-and-white packaging is flashing in the corner of my eye, hypnotising me, lulling me into loving them even more than I already do and convincing me that their purchase is essential to my happiness.

My lunch comes to less than £3 and the present I'm buying myself as a reward for not buying anything is nearly £30.

Even I can see that doesn't add up.

The spell is broken, the basket stops swinging and the boxes go back.

Friday 13 October – Day 152

Redemption!

After telling Kevin about my near miss, he informs me that he needs deodorant from Clarins and if I get him two, then I can pick up the freebies.

I love that man!

Saturday 14 October – Day 153

The days are getting colder and darker, prompting me to think of hibernating – insulating myself with layers of fabulous winter fashion – but it's not to be.

This autumn there'll be no kitting myself out in preparation for the big freeze. No new boots, no new coat, gloves or scarves.

The only winter wear I'll be working is the stuff from last year that's still hanging in the wardrobe. But that's the whole point – it's all still there and half of it's hardly been worn, if at all.

Before I even look, I can tell you there are four full-length coats in there, one that's never been out of the wrapper. And the boots … flat, heeled, wedged, suede, leather, black, brown, green and pure white fur (fake of course!).

The latter I had seen in a magazine, whiter than the snow they were pictured on, and I knew they were the boots that would make my winter magical. After a campaign that would have impressed the Bush party, I persuaded Kevin to buy them for my birthday. Then the weather turned nasty …

I couldn't bring myself to defile them on the damp dirty pavements, but by the time the weather had changed for the better, they'd gone high street and were adorning the feet of every gum-chewing, crop-topped teenager.

(I did wear them once … to a fancy-dress party and even then I carried them there in a bag, and changed into them on the doorstep so they didn't get dirty.)

Sunday 15 October – Day 154
Thinking about my boots yesterday reminded me of another white-fur fiasco in my life.

When I was a child I had a coat, hat and muffler all in white fur. Apparently my parents thought I looked 'cute' in it, but as I had ginger hair as a child, the only thing I looked 'cute' in was a balaclava!

Anyway, my mother had decked me out in my furry fin-est and dashed off to fetch her bag, leaving me alone in the kitchen with the immortal words: 'Don't touch that jar.'

I hadn't even noticed the jar until she said that, but it immediately became the most important and irresistible thing I'd ever seen.

Two minutes later, she runs back to find a screaming beet-root of a child, covered from head to toe in bright red powder – jewellers rouge. Impossible to remove, even with the copi-ous amount of tears I was shedding.

Needless to say, the backs of my legs were as red as my coat after my mother had finished with me.

Monday 16 October – Day 155

Kevin has arrived home with a crash helmet.

A naughty spin on the pillion on a quiet back road has given him the bug and now he's expecting me to drive him everywhere.

I do everything I can to get out of it, finally coming up with the highly plausible: 'My insurance will go up and I can't afford the extra payments.'

But when I call the insurance agents, they say they'll happily cover me to carry a passenger at no additional cost. Damn! The one time I actually was hoping they'd whack on a couple of hundred quid.

I have no more excuses left, so off we go, wobbling along at twenty miles an hour, with Kevin whooping and hollering on the back.

He's only silenced when we're passed by a man on a bicycle.

Tuesday 17 October – Day 156

I don't feel well.

Part of me thinks it may be a bug and part of me thinks it's psychosomatic as I just can't be bothered starting the decluttering I promised myself I'd do today.

After exhausting myself with every gardening/cookery/priceless-work-of-art-in-your-loft programme, I grab a pad and start noting down all the things I need to do.

Things to throw out, things to sell, things to recycle, things to shred, things to save money on. Endless things! No wonder my head hurts.

Kevin comes home to find me sulking in the lounge, surrounded by all of the bits of paper and notes that I've written for myself.

Wearing my best feeling-sorry-for-myself face, I look up at him, hoping for sympathy.

'What's wrong?' he asks, flicking through the wads of paper and trying to stifle his laughter. 'Are you feeling a bit listless?'

He just manages to make it to the door before I lob the whole lot at him.

Wednesday 18 October – Day 157

I've managed to drag my disease-ridden carcass off the couch and have started clearing out some of my clothes.

A bold move for someone who can't buy any new ones, but now that I'm not so consumed with consumerism and have stopped to take stock, the quantity of stuff I have is completely overwhelming.

My earlier clear-out came to a paltry four bags that were destined for eBay. But the lack of a digital camera means they've been gathering dust in the study for the past few months. The only saving grace is that these bags have remained closed. Usually I sneak back into them and before I know it, there's a solo sock left for the benefit of the charity shop.

I need to scale down so that I can see some of the precious purchases hanging in my wardrobe and maybe even get round to wearing a few.

When you have as many clothes as I do, the easiest way to plan what you're wearing is to grab whatever's on top of the ironing pile. It's just too much hassle to plough through all of those other skirts, shirts, trousers, dresses and jumpers and try to put together a look.

And that's the irony of the whole thing. Despite the fact that I could probably wear a different outfit every day for a year without ever wearing the same ensemble twice, I find myself in the same clothes time after time.

A classic case of not being able to see the (Vivienne West)wood for the trees.

Thursday 19 October – Day 158

I grab a quick coffee with Verity today, in a bid to cram in as much cake and gossiping as possible before her baby arrives. There's more gossiping than cramming though as her bump is taking up much of her cake capacity.

Our coffee consumption starts at my place, where Hobbs decides to use her tummy as a trampoline. She endures nearly half an hour of him bouncing around and springing as high as he can to get a good lick at her face, before we come to the conclusion that going out is a better and more peaceful option.

We talk about the perverse pleasures of wearing out clothes and finishing off bottles of shampoo, shower gel and the like. The satisfaction you get from squeezing that last drop out before rushing to rinse the bottle and chuck it in the recycling. The elation of eking out the final wear of a garment that was once so vibrant and that's now resigned to seeing out its days as a duster.

Admittedly, it's been years since I've done the latter, but strangely it's something I'm looking forward to.

Friday 20 October – Day 159
Kevin has managed to borrow a digital camera!

We spend the evening positioning, primping and preening all of the things that I've promised to sell. I even drag out three of my Mulberry bags, although it's breaking my heart to even think about parting with them.

They look so gorgeous that I'm worried I'll log on to eBay myself and try to buy them back.

Saturday 21 October – Day 160
'The Fear' has kicked in!

I knew it would happen sooner rather than later, but still I wasn't fully prepared for it.

I'd been happily minding my own business, trundling round the flat finding excuses not to do the dusting, when suddenly I felt the hairs on the back of my neck lifting.

There, on the radio were the first familiar bars of ... a Christmas song!

Suddenly I was sweating – stressing about what to buy, where to buy it, how to pay for it.

Two decades of debt have reprogrammed me, rendering me unable to enjoy the festive season without fear.

I loved Christmas when I was younger and now I'm so miserable, I could give Scrooge a run for his money. What happened to the person that used to leave out biscuits for Rudolph and a whisky for Santa Claus?

Okay, so she stopped doing that aged ten after finding her parents making icing-sugar prints on the fireplace and putting two and two together, but maybe this year could see a return of a little of that Christmas cheer – on the cheap.

It's bye-bye Bah Humbug and hello Holly Wreath.

Sunday 22 October – Day 161

Walking Hobbs today, I'm amazed by the amount of new flats springing up in the area, but even more amazed by their prices.

Flats starting at £198,000! I know in the heart of London that would be seen as the best bargain ever, but this is Scotland and here the average wage is around £26,000, so who can afford these properties?

It's not as if they aren't being bought. When I look more closely at the map of the unfinished site, there are only a handful of flats that haven't been snapped up.

Are there multitudes of people out there getting themselves deeper and deeper into debt for the sake of a plush pad, extending the length of their mortgages to the point that they'll never be able to retire?

My debt suddenly seems tiny in comparison to the 50-year mortgage deal that so many first-time buyers are opting for.

Monday 23 October – Day 162

Our neighbour, Helen, calls to tell us that her partner's mother has died.

Two months ago, Sarah's sister died and Helen had planned a holiday that would take her away from it all. They were four days into that holiday when the news about Sarah's